# FOUR
# REFORMERS

396

# FOUR REFORMERS
## Luther▪Melanchthon▪Calvin▪Zwingli

# KURT ALAND

Translated by James L. Schaaf

**AUGSBURG** Publishing House • Minneapolis

Manufactured in the United States of America

# Contents

# Preface

For decades there has not been a comprehensive presentation of the reformers from a single pen. This book attempts to fulfill this need. It also became evident that such a presentation could not—as was usual in earlier generations—be limited to Luther, Calvin, and Zwingli, but that Melanchthon also had to be included. It was also considered necessary to add a postscript to show that the title of "Reformer" applies not only to the four men discussed here and that the Reformation was not merely a German or Swiss event, but that it was a movement involving all of Europe. It was appropriate to the nature of the volume to add a discussion of some contemporary problems. Although this work deals with the past, it is a past whose power extends into the present. One may only wish that its significance continue to increase.

For this edition by Augsburg Publishing House the text of the German publication has been amplified or clarified in a number of places. I am indebted to my colleague

James L. Schaaf for his translation which makes this presentation accessible to new areas, an action that is extremely significant because the Reformation has long since transcended its original European form and significance and has become an international force whose effects have often exceeded those in its original centers.

# Martin Luther

*Martin Luther was born November 10, 1483, in Eis-
leben, the second son of Hans Luther, a miner and
later small mining contractor, and his wife Margarete
Lindemann. After the family moved to Mansfeld
(1484) he attended school there (after 1488), and later
in Magdeburg and Eisenach (1498). In April, 1501, he
began his studies at the University of Erfurt, and
earned the Bachelor of Arts in 1502 and Master of
Arts in 1505. On July 17, 1505, he entered the Erfurt
monastery of the Augustinian Hermits as a novice,
and in 1507 was ordained a priest and began the study
of theology.*

*In the autumn of 1508, he was assigned to teach at the
University of Wittenberg; in 1510 he made a trip to
Rome on behalf of the order; in 1511 he was transferred back to Wittenberg where he earned the Doctor
of Theology degree on October 19, 1512, and on the
following day became a professor on the theological
faculty. Until his death he discharged the responsibility
of his position* as Lectura in Biblia *(in which he was*

*preceded by Staupitz) by lecturing on biblical books.
The lectures from 1513-1518 (first series on the Psalms,
on Romans, Galatians, and Hebrews) and the lectures
from the 1535-1545 years (on Genesis) are the most
important.*

*On October 31, 1517, he posted* Ninety-five Theses
Concerning Indulgences *and initiated the rapidly-
growing indulgence controversy. In 1520 he wrote the
so-called chief reformatory writings:* To the Christian
Nobility of the German Nation, The Babylonian Captivity of the Church, *and* The Freedom of a Christian.
*A bull threatening to excommunicate Luther was pre-
pared by the pope on June 15, 1520, and was burned
by Luther on December 10 of the same year. The excommunication, however, took effect January 3, 1521.
He appeared at the Diet of Worms on April 16-18, 1521,
and was placed under the imperial ban on May 8, 1521.
At the Wartburg in 1521 he translated the New Testament into German (published as the "September" Testament in 1522), and from that time worked continually
on translating the Bible and revising his earlier work
(even after the appearance of the entire Bible in 1534).
Impelled by the unrest in Wittenberg, he returned
there in the spring of 1522 and only infrequently left
the city during the remainder of his life (in 1529 to
the Marburg Colloquy, in 1537 to the conference in
Smalcald, and in 1545-1546 to Eisleben to mediate the
disputes between the counts of Mansfeld).*

*The center of his life was his professorship (from
which he received his salary, refusing all honoraria
for his writings) and his preaching activity, plus in-
numerable letters and other writings, all directed to
concrete situations. On June 13, 1525, he married a
former nun, Katherina von Bora, who bore the follow-*

*ing children: Hans in 1526 (in 1530 the Letter to Little*
*Hans Luther), Elisabeth in 1528, Magdalene in 1529,*
*Paul in 1533, and Margarete in 1534. He died in Eis-*
*leben on February 18, 1546 (probably of angina pec-*
*toris), and on February 22, 1546, was buried in the*
*Castle Church in Wittenberg.*

～～～～～～～～～～～～

Each year at least five hundred new publications on the
subject of Martin Luther and the Reformation appear,
written in a wide variety of languages. Although Luther
research was previously the domain of German scholarship,
today no one can get along without a knowledge of the
work on the sixteenth century being done especially in
Scandinavia, the United States, and England. Despite the
scope and depth of this work, however, no one has yet
produced a modern equivalent to the Luther biography of
Köstlin-Kawerau which last appeared in 1905; [1] Scheel's
attempt to do so ended with a presentation of Luther's first
activity in Wittenberg.[2] Köstlin-Kawerau almost completely
neglected the decisively important early lectures of Luther,
which first became available in the twentieth century,[3] and
Scheel's work did not advance far enough to treat them.
Likewise the existing presentations of Luther's complete
theology are either outdated or unsatisfactory, and the
numerous monographs cannot fill the breach.

This illuminates the current situation concerning scholarly work on Luther. There appears to be much less work
done by non-specialists than earlier, which is all the more
regrettable since there is apparently considerable interest in
the Reformation. The popular presentation of Luther by
Richard Friedenthal [4] has appeared in a printing of several

hundred thousand copies, dramas in which Luther plays a leading role are frequently performed in England (John Osborne)[5] and Germany (Dieter Forte),[6] and textbooks appear in many editions and are translated into other languages. The interest in Luther even extends into the sphere of genuine literature; the last writing on which Thomas Mann was working was to be a play, *Luther's Marriage*.[7]

This work was never completed. It would have considerably altered the position which Thomas Mann adopted in his speeches and articles about Luther and the Reformation (e.g., "Germany and the Germans"[8] in 1945, and "The Three Mighty Ones"[9] in 1949), for at the end of his life Thomas Mann had met the historical Luther and through his study of important literature and sources had changed his earlier opinions and prejudices. The Luther one finds in the plays of Osborne and Forte has, despite all the dramatic scenes and dialog they contain, only little (Osborne) or absolutely nothing at all (Forte) to do with the historical Luther. Osborne proceeds on the basis of Erik H. Erikson's book *Young Man Luther*, and its conclusions from depth psychology,[10] that rest on insufficient (and often frivolously interpreted) data. For Forte, Luther is simply a puppet manipulated by his elector Frederick the Wise through the court chaplain Spalatin so that Frederick can get the treasures of the church for himself. Forte sees the Reformation itself as a means of achieving and consolidating the power of capitalism which is represented by the Fuggers.[11] The fact that both plays have enjoyed such extraordinary public acclaim simply shows how little the public knows about the real Luther and the facts of the Reformation.

In regard to Luther, the situation has become less complicated. One group whose thought and judgment was previously dominated by cliches has completely changed and a second group shows at least signs of weakening. "Almost all (Roman Catholic) Luther literature from Luther's death until well into the twentieth century," testifies Adolf Herte, [12] "has followed the course of only one work," the *Commentaria de actis et scriptis Martini Lutheri* of Johannes Cochlaeus, [13] which first appeared in 1549. In this work, produced in the struggle against the Reformation, a picture of Luther appeared which had nothing positive about it, except for occasional references to his endeavors as a monk. In the whole realm of the Catholic church this excessive polemic has been demolished since World War II through a new dialog and a new understanding between the two confessions. Even though it may not be as fully developed as one might wish, Catholic research on the Reformation is well on the way to providing its special contribution toward greater clarity and a greater understanding of the Reformation period, and this is sure to be an absolutely necessary corrective to a certain Protestant one-sidedness and bias.

A good deal more recent, but also much more entrenched are the Marxist judgments of Luther; in their one-sidedness they almost surpass the Catholic critics of an earlier age. The party line of orthodox Marxism was set by Friedrich Engels' *The Peasant War in Germany,* written in 1850. According to Engels, "when in 1517 opposition against the dogmas and organisation of the Catholic Church was first raised by Luther," he took a totally revolutionary stance. But this "revolutionary ardour" did not last long. For the peasants and plebians, Luther's "preaching of Christian freedom" sounded the signal for a revolutionary uprising that would "wreak vengeance upon all their oppressors."

However, "the moderate middle-class and a large section of
the lower nobility," and also the princes who followed Luther, wanted only to break the power of the Catholic
hierarchy and their dependence on Rome, "and enrich
themselves through the confiscation of church property."

Eventually Luther was forced to choose between these
two parties. "Luther, the protégé of the Elector of Saxony,
the respected professor of Wittenberg who had become
powerful and famous overnight, and was surrounded by a
coterie of servile creatures and flatterers, did not hesitate a
moment. He dropped the popular elements of the movement, and joined the train of the middle-class, the nobility
and the princes." Then the cry for a war to annihilate Rome
was stilled, and instead Luther began to preach peaceful
development and passive resistance. When Hutten invited
him to visit Sickingen, i.e., to come into the "centre of the
noble conspiracy against clergy and princes," Luther
refused; it was not by force, but by the Word that the rule
of the gospel must triumph. At that moment began the
disgusting "bartering and haggling" which in 1530 led to
the Augsburg Confession, the "constitution of the reformed
middle-class church."

Luther was not only a "recognized representative of
middle-class reform," but also, by increasingly distancing
himself from the radical wing, he "fell more and more
under the control of the reformed princes." Very early
"Luther's subservience to them increased." As the Peasants'
War broke out in 1525, mostly in Catholic territories, Luther
sought to take a mediating position and "resolutely attacked
the governments." But as the revolt spread to Protestant territories and the danger that "middle-class reform would
have been swept away by the tides of a peasant-plebeian

revolution" increased, "there was no more time for circumspection." In *Against the Robbing and Murderous Hordes of Peasants* Luther gave his express blessing to every possible means of cruel extermination. With his translation of the Bible Luther "had given the plebeian movement a powerful weapon," for in it a society was depicted which had no trace of a feudal hierarchy. Now Luther turned the Bible against the peasants and extracted from it "a veritable hymn to the authorities ordained by God—a feat hardly exceeded by any lackey of absolute monarchy." With this justification of the existing order, including serfdom, Luther denied his early years and betrayed to the princes not only the radical element, but even the middle-class wing of the Reformation.[14]

All of this was written by Engels not as a historical study, but as a polemic in the political arguments of his day; for all factual material, according to his own testimony, he relied on the *Allgemeine Geschichte des grossen Bauernkrieges,* published in 1841-1843 by Wilhelm Zimmerman, an alleged theologian. Nevertheless it soon attained something like canonical significance. From Franz Mehring[15] and Karl Kautsky[16] to the present, one finds Engels' assessment of Luther again and again in Marxist studies of the Reformation, often repeated verbatim. Only in recent times have Soviet historians (e.g., M. M. Smirin)[17] taken the lead in suggesting that something beyond Engels is needed to come to an understanding of Luther and the Reformation. Slowly a more just and factual evaluation of Luther is spreading;[18] characteristic of this is the title of Gerhard Zschäbitz's book in 1967, *Martin Luther, Grösse und Grenze* ("magnitude and limit").

It goes without saying that in this view, which we will not discuss here, Thomas Müntzer is the real hero and the personification of what the Reformation originally intended. This has not changed and it may take a long time before the change in the position of the leading Marxist historians filters down to the grassroots. Ernst Block's position, unchanged since 1921, [19] and Forte's play about Luther, are eloquent examples, for here Engels' way of thinking is still normative, even in exaggerated form. Yet the growing changes have significant implications.

If one is to speak about Martin Luther, it would be most appropriate to do it in dialog with the contemporary discussion, whether it is theological or secular in nature. Martin Luther's childhood is the place to begin. In contrast to people like Erikson, Osborne, and others who make a great deal of father-son conflicts, identity crises, etc., one must maintain that this childhood—measured by the standards of that age—was quite normal. When Luther reports in his *Table Talk* (which was recorded much later, not until after 1531) that his mother beat him for stealing a nut until blood flowed, [20] and that his father once paddled him so much that Luther was "worried that he might not win me back again," [21] these are the exceptions, not the rule.  That is why these events were so impressed on Luther's memory. If we attempt to draw conclusions about Luther's attitude to his parents from these events, we are bound to err. If we also look at the other facts and statements that have been preserved, especially Luther's letters to his parents, we find a loving relationship of a son to his parents. It is no wonder that the household was run with absolute frugality for the sake of social advancement; the father's expenditures for the optimum education of his son, who was chosen to advance to the next highest social class—the educator—speak clearly.

It was the father's intention that his son should become a lawyer, i.e., perhaps an advisor of one of the many governmental authorities. There were plans for suitable marriage as a "flanking maneuver" for the social ascent of the son and thus of the family. But these plans were destroyed by Martin Luther's entrance into the Augustinian order, to the complete despair of his father and the entire family. How was such a thing possible? The son had grown up in the traditional faith permeating the family home. We certainly cannot claim that any sort of dislike or animosity toward the church existed, although occasionally such claims have been advanced.

Yet not until his days in Eisenach, where for several years Luther lived in close association with the patrician families of Schalbe and Cotta and with the monks of the Carmelite monastery, did he enter the sphere of a living piety, and at the same time became acquainted with the way higher-class people lived. This late medieval piety was indeed filled with anxiety and fear. It dreaded death and strove with all its might to be reconciled with a God who severely punished sin. This attitude explains why the veneration of saints flourished, why so many foundations were established and why so many pilgrimages took place, and why there was such an enormous development of the various forms of indulgences. Yet despite all that, the step of entering a monastery—which Luther took on July 17, 1505—was still an exception, regardless of the growth of monasteries. In some way or another, ordinary people of that day would find their inner peace through the usual comforts of the church and would not resort to the final alternative, the "evangelical life" of the monk, even though the general understanding was that the monastic life, rightly lived, would guarantee eternal bliss.

The external cause of Luther's decision was the event at Stotternheim on July 2, 1505. While returning from a visit to his parents, Luther had almost reached Erfurt when a thunderstorm caught him. As a lightning bolt struck near him, he involuntarily cried out, "St. Anne, help me. I will become a monk." [22] This is the gist of the report which has become embellished with many legends. Luther was certainly aware that a thunderstorm was a natural occurrence, yet at Stotternheim he definitely felt that God was calling him personally. The danger of a sudden death while he was unprepared—despite the church's practice of confession and extreme unction—forced this vow from him now, although in his heart he had obviously been on the way toward it.

Melanchthon, who was not especially informed about all the circumstances surrounding the episode, was certainly correct when he reported that the fear of God's wrath and his judgment drove Luther into the monastery.[23] Actually this was not a sufficient reason. Luther had successfully completed his studies. He had earned both the Bachelor and Master of Arts in the shortest time possible, and had ranked second in a class of seventeen candidates for the latter degree. In this way he had earned the right to teach the "seven liberal arts" and to continue his studies in one of the higher faculties, in his case that of law. In the summer semester of 1505 he had begun on schedule, but suddenly interrupted his studies to make a visit to his home. This is the only indication that something was "out of order." Exactly what it was has been the object of much discussion, but the sources give us no direct answer. Indirect conclusions may be drawn from Luther's actions in the weeks following the event at Stotternheim.

According to the rules, ways and means would have been open to Luther to revoke his decision to enter the monastery. If someone would have suggested to him that he had promised merely to enter the monastery, i.e., to spend a year as a novice and not to remain a monk for his entire life, such an argument might have been reasonable, but completely unacceptable casuistry to anyone who took the questions of life and faith seriously. It was different with the completely justified objection that in the moment of making his vow Luther was not in possession of the freedom of choice, so that according to law it was invalid. Luther made no use of these avenues of escape. He did indeed speak later of the fact that he became a monk "by force," not "happily and of my own free will," and that he regretted his vow.[24] He even hesitated for two weeks, but then he appeared at the gate of the monastery of the Augustinian Hermits in Erfurt. His renewed self-examination had resulted in the unavoidable consequences of his vow at Stotternheim; what had been working inside him, but had not been brought to conclusion, finally broke through.

Luther's monastic period is filled with numerous legends, Catholic as well as Evangelical. If only a tiny portion of what Catholic polemics have maintained about Luther's novitiate were true, he would never have been allowed to make his profession as a monk, an act which required examination by the prior and the members of the order of the novice's character, and which occurred without difficulty for him at the conclusion of his probationary period. Father Luther enjoyed a good reputation in the Erfurt monastery. As soon as he had made his profession, he was instructed to prepare for entrance into the priesthood, and after his ordination as a priest in 1507 he was admitted to study theology. During this period of theological study he was transferred in 1508 to the University at Wittenberg to be an instructor in the faculty of arts there. On his return to Erfurt he continued his lecturing, now in the faculty of theology.

When it appeared that the austerity of the order was in danger of being modified, the protesting monasteries sent a two-man delegation to Rome in 1510. Erfurt was entitled to name one of the pair, and chose as its spokesman Father Luther, which indicates that he was not only a spokesman for the strict group, but that he also enjoyed an uncontested authority among his brethren. Luther also held offices in the monastery, another proof of his reputation. After his permanent transfer to Wittenberg in 1511 he was soon named subprior and monastery preacher, and in 1515 he became district vicar of his order with supervision over ten, and later eleven monasteries in Meissen and Thuringia. He conducted this office with utmost conscientiousness and carefulness.

But the Protestant tales about Luther's wretched and even disgraceful treatment in the monastery are also legends, even though they may have originated only a few decades after his death. Luther certainly did criticize his time as a monk most severely, but it was never because of his brethren. It was rather because of the torments imposed by the monastic life, or (one could also say) imposed by Luther on himself. It is not that Luther did not have moments of exhilaration. One of them was doubtless the festive meal after his ordination as a priest in 1507, at which he attempted to depict for his father the "divine life" of the monk, in the mistaken assumption that his father had become reconciled to his decision. Hans Luther's reference to parental obedience demanded by the fourth command-ment and his question whether the Stotternheim experience had not been a phantasm, helped to destroy this feeling of exhilaration.[25] Both these things had an ongoing impact on Luther, especially since he already had a decisive experience the first time he celebrated mass. Here when he stood for the first time in the presence of God's majesty performing the sacred mystery, a deep, completely confusing fear came over him. One may well say that the first part of Luther's monastic experience was filled with great expectations and hopes; he wanted to make full use of the opportunity to come to terms with God which was offered him there.

During his novitiate year his freedom of activity was limited, for everything he did was determined by the master of the novices, of whom Luther later testified that he had been "an excellent man and a true Christian under the damned cowl."[26] After he made his profession this limitation was removed. Luther devoted himself excessively to all the ecclesiastical means which were designed to make one "righteous before God," which meant leading a sinless, God-pleasing life in accordance with his commandments. "It is true that I was a pious monk and followed the rules of my order so faithfully that I may say, if ever a man could have entered heaven through monkery it would have been I. All my comrades in the monastery who knew me would testify to that. And if I had had the time I would have martyred myself with vigils, prayers, readings, and other works,"[27] Luther declared in retrospect in 1533, to cite only one of his many pertinent statements. God de-mands nothing of us that we cannot do, and if we do what is in our power, God will reward our efforts—that was

Luther's conviction, fully in accordance with his theological teachers and the general view of his day. But even when he had diligently confessed all his sins and his confessor had absolved him, still Luther felt just as much a sinner as before. Equally futile for him were all the other works commanded or counseled by the church. When this happened he did not make the regulations of the church responsible for his lack of inner satisfaction, but looked for the cause in his failure to perform the ecclesiastical regulations satisfactorily and thus increased his works. The tormenting thought of predestination added to his woes. If God, on the basis of his foreknowledge of our actions, had destined one person for salvation and another for condemnation (as the contemporary religious view taught), Luther could do nothing on the basis of his experiences but consider himself among the condemned.

His torments grew and grew. As though speaking of another person, he reported in 1518 in his *Explanations of the Ninety-five Theses:*

> I myself "knew a man" who claimed that he had often suffered these punishments, in fact over a very brief period of time. Yet they were so great and so much like hell that no tongue could adequately express them, no pen could describe them, and one who had not himself experienced them could not believe them. And so great were they that, if they had been sustained or had lasted for half an hour, even for one tenth of an hour, he would have perished completely and all of his bones would have been reduced to ashes. At such a time God seems terribly angry, and with him the whole creation. At such a time there is no flight, no comfort, within or without, but all things accuse.[28]

That was Luther in the monastery. His struggle for a "gracious God" led him to hate the "righteous God," who set his own righteousness as the standard for us and never let us attain this righteousness. In an autobiographical reminiscence of 1545 he wrote:

> Though I lived as a monk without reproach, I felt that I was a sinner before God with an extremely disturbed conscience. I could not believe that he was placated by my satisfaction. I did not love, yes, I hated the righteous God who punishes sinners, and secretly, if not blasphemously, certainly murmuring greatly, I was angry with God, and said, "As if, indeed, it is not enough, that miserable sinners, eternally lost through original sin, are crushed by every kind of calamity by the law of the decalogue, without having God add pain to pain by the gospel and also by the gospel threatening us with his righteousness and wrath!" [29]

A passage in Romans 1:17 assumed central significance in Luther's struggle: "For in it [the gospel] the righteousness of God is revealed." He had hated this word, says Luther in 1545, "which according to the use and custom of all the teachers, I had been taught to understand philosophically regarding the formal or active righteousness, as they called it, with which God is righteous and punishes the unrighteous sinner." Again and again he wrestled with this word "with a fierce and troubled conscience," until God finally had mercy upon him and let him see that it did not refer to active righteousness, but to passive righteousness, i.e., that which God gives through faith. Day and night he had puzzled over this, Luther reports, but now "I felt that I was altogether born again and had entered paradise itself through open gates." He ran through the Scriptures from memory to test this new insight and found it confirmed everywhere. "And I extolled my sweetest word with a love as great as the hatred with which I had before hated the word 'righteousness of God.' Thus that place in Paul was for me truly the gate to paradise." [30]

This is the way Luther describes the dawn of his Reformation consciousness, the so-called "tower experience." Where it took place cannot be disputed (it was in the heated study room in the tower of the monastery Luther occupied as subprior), but the date it happened has become a topic of lively debate. Although in his autobiographical reminiscence Luther speaks unambiguously of a time shortly before his second series of lectures on the Psalms, i.e., 1518, Protestant research has generally looked at this as the mistaken recollection of an old man and preferred to date the tower experience earlier than that. Different scholars assigned different dates, but they all placed it early enough that several years lay between it and the beginning of the indulgence controversy in 1517. Today, however, scholars are more and more coming to the conclusion that Luther's recollection was correct and that the dawning of the Reformation consciousness should be dated in the spring of 1518. [31]

The extensive debate on this topic was not merely an idle dispute about chronology, but it implied a fundamental shift in the interpretation of his early lectures, which previously had been considered a complete expression of Luther's theology and had often been the exclusive subject material considered in numerous studies. Indeed, it meant a shift in the entire interpretation and evaluation of the reformer and his development. According to the "early dating," it was necessary to postulate "Years of

Silence" (as a chapter of a well-known Luther biography put it)[32] between the Reformation breakthrough and its consequences for theology and the church, a conception that might make sense for a modern professor, but not for the historical Luther and the vehement character of his struggle. The "late dating" offers a comprehensive and logical picture of the reformer's development that is the only way one can explain, for example, the "explosion" in his literary activity from 1518 on. In addition to the theological treatises and polemic articles which were necessary because of the dispute about indulgences, there now appeared "a constant and frequent stream of German devotional works entirely non-polemical, and exclusively concerned with what makes a man a Christian." [33] From the previous period there exists only one single writing, his *Exposition of the Penitential Psalms* of 1517.

When Luther assumed the position of *Lectura in Biblia* which Staupitz had held on the Wittenberg theological faculty, he had the usual training in the Occamist scholastic tradition and in addition he possessed a great rarity at that time, an intimate knowledge of the text of the entire Bible, a knowledge which dated back to the first years of his monastery experience and was strengthened by intensive reading. Moreover, since 1509 he had been exposed to Augustine, especially his writings in the Pelagian and Semi-pelagian controversies, and Luther made these writings and the theological position embodied in them more and more his own. This too was by no means the rule in his day. For example, in January, 1517, his colleague Karlstadt traveled to Leipzig to buy an edition of Augustine's works for his continuing study, hoping that he could refute Luther from its contents. Karlstadt's actual study of the Scriptures began much later. Nearly all those elements in Luther's early lectures which give the impression of anything reformatory come almost exclusively from Augustine's anti-Pelagian writings, or from those statements of St. Paul which Luther exegeted (except when he delivered his first series of lectures on the Psalms).

Characteristic of this period of Luther's development are the series of theses he prepared for Bernhardi in 1516 *(Concerning the Power and Will of Man without Grace)* [34] and Günther in 1517 *(Against Scholastic Theology),* [35] and even to a certain degree the theses for the Heidelberg Disputation which were written at the beginning of 1518.[36] We should not claim that the Reformation breakthrough was an isolated event which brought in something absolutely new with no connection to what went before; the preparation for it was laid in many individual steps. "For a long time I went astray and didn't know what I was about. To be sure, I knew something, but I didn't know what it was until I came to the text in Romans 1:17. . . . I made myself free,"[37] said Luther in his *Table Talk* concerning his development. To use a figurative analogy, Luther's lectures, disputations, and other writings before 1518 are like the sky in springtime, filled with clouds but through which the sun shines from time to time.

The "early dating" rests on the isolated interpretation of individual passages, but when their context and the lectures as a whole are considered the conclusion is quite different. Luther's attitude toward Augustine, when he reread *The Spirit and the Letter* after the Reformation breakthrough, is characteristic. He was surprised to find righteousness defined here in a way similar to his new understanding, yet he found that here Augustine "spoke imperfectly and he

did not express all things . . . clearly." [38] In his early lectures
Luther made considerable use of this writing without being
aware of this aspect, simply because his consciousness had
not yet made the decisive change. When that happened, he
was amazed to find the same thought in Augustine, whom
his own development had meanwhile left behind.

It was Luther's conviction that the Reformation—the
"Lutheran rumpus"—had begun with the controversy over
indulgences.[39] Luther knew nothing about the financial
dealings between Rome, the Fuggers, and Albrecht of
Mainz that stood behind the "reconciliation with God" for
the living and the dead, penitent and impenitent, which
Tetzel was proclaiming. What moved him to prepare the
*Ninety-five Theses* was rather Tetzel's blasphemous talk
and the internal destruction of the Wittenberg congregation. As he posted them on the door of the Wittenberg
Castle Church (which the university used as its bulletin
board) on October 31, 1517—a fact which despite much
argumentation,[40] cannot be doubted—he had no idea that
they would soon echo throughout Germany, especially since
his even sharper *Disputation Against Scholastic Theology* a
few weeks earlier had, notwithstanding all his efforts, fallen
on deaf ears. There is no doubt that Luther at that time
stood in complete devotion to the Catholic church and that
he thought that the misuse of these indulgences was occur-
ring without the knowledge of Albrecht of Mainz and the
church itself (for the church had never officially defined the
matter of indulgences); only modern people looking back
at the event could view it differently. At that time Luther
was a devout Catholic and a passionate defender of the
church and the papacy, as he acknowledged in his autobiographical statement of 1545 ("a monk and a most en-

thusiastic papist . . . so drunk, yes submerged in the pope's dogmas . . . not such a lump of frigid ice in defending the papacy as Eck and his like").[41]

Luther did not plan the Reformation ahead of time and then work to accomplish it (as Zwingli did). He was drawn into it by force, he later stated, like a horse wearing blinders.[42] On October 31, 1517, he obediently sent the *Ninety-five Theses* to Albrecht of Mainz,[43] and in June, 1518, he obediently sent his *Explanations of the Ninety-five Theses* to Pope Leo X ("Make alive or kill, refute, approve or disapprove as it pleases you; your voice I shall recognize as the voice of Christ who directs and speaks through you").[44] But Rome's answer was the *Dialogue* of Prierias (who stated with regard to indulgences that anyone who said that the Roman church could not do what it was doing was a heretic) and the initiation of legal proceedings against the heretic.

It was complications in imperial politics that kept the prosecution from being implemented immediately. Emperor Maximilian was ill and his successor needed to be chosen. In this process Luther's ruler, Elector Frederick the Wise, played an important and increasingly significant role until he himself became the curia's leading candidate for the highest office of the empire. Because this was recognized, Luther was examined initially by Cardinal Cajetan, the papal legate, in October, 1518, during the meeting of the imperial diet in Augsburg, instead of in Rome. Then there were continual delays until the election of Charles V in 1519 made it no longer necessary to treat the elector with care, and a papal bull threatening excommunication *(Exsurge Domine)* was signed in June, 1520, after much too hasty preparation.

But the Luther who appeared before Cajetan was a different Luther than the one who had written the *Explanations*. Now he had gone through the tower experience (his dedication of the *Explanations* to Staupitz clearly shows that Luther had not yet attained the Reformation consciousness when the indulgence controversy began in 1517).[45] He passionately opposed the cardinal. And the Luther who received the bull threatening excommunication was still a different man. For by that time he had fought through the Leipzig Debate in July, 1519, in which Eck had provoked him into making judgments about the limited authority of the papacy and church councils, which Luther had indeed been thinking about, but had not yet come to a firm conclusion.[46] It is true that he had written to Spalatin in March, 1519, in connection with his preparation for the debate: "And, confidentially, I do not know whether the pope is the Antichrist himself or whether he is his apostle, so miserably (this is the truth) is Christ corrupted and crucified by the pope in his decretals."[47] But it took many more attacks from his opponents and the papal bull itself to convince him of this thought; if he were right, the bond which still held him tightly to the Catholic church would finally be severed.

After laying the groundwork in his sermons during 1519, Luther produced his three reformatory treatises of 1520, in which he first demolished the "three walls" the Romanists had erected to guard their own privileges: That spiritual power is superior to temporal, that only the pope can interpret Scripture, and that the pope alone has the right to summon a general council. The restoration of the early church's priesthood of all believers breaks down all these walls. Each Christian is truly a priest and possesses all the powers of a priest; believers are different from one another only in the function they have to perform. Thus everyone has the right to interpret the Scriptures and even to call a council if there is need for one. The temporal authorities are in the best position to do this not simply because of the position of authority they hold, but chiefly because of their task to guard against evil. In his writing *To the Christian Nobility of the German Nation Regarding the Reform of the Christian Estate*,[48] Luther, after introducing this subject, provides the nobility with a long list of topics that ought to be considered by a future church council, powerfully summarizing the vexations and complaints that Germany had had against the Catholic church for generations. A few weeks later he went even further and spoke about *The Babylonian Captivity of the Church*.[49] Just as the Jews were once in captivity in Babylon, today it is the true Christians who are captive because the Antichrist has robbed the church of its freedom by falsely evaluating and interpreting the sacraments.

Only Baptism and the Lord's Supper fulfill the scriptural requirements for a sacrament: Promise and accompanying sign. Penance has the promise but not the sign, and really is associated with Baptism. All the other "sacraments"—confirmation, marriage, ordination, and extreme unction—are inventions of later times and have occasioned numerous abuses. The biblical references intended to prove their institution have all been misunderstood. For example, extreme unction was based on James 5:14, but the anointing mentioned there is for the purpose of healing the sick person, not preparing him for death. The sacramental character of marriage was based on Ephesians 5:32. But there the text speaks only of a mystery *(mysterion* in Greek). Although the early Latin translation rendered this with the word *sacramentum* (whose meaning at that time was the equivalent of *mysterion*), this was far from establishing the sacramental character of marriage. Even the Lord's Supper and Baptism, just like penance, had to be restored from the damage done to them by the Catholic church if they were to regain their old power. All of this Luther described as only a "prelude" to the recantation which he had heard that Rome would be demanding of him.

When this demand for his recantation within 60 days appeared in the papal bull *Exsurge Domine,* Luther progressed to the conclusion that had been developing in his mind since 1519: The papacy was the Antichrist. The temporal authority it had assumed, as well as its claim that its power over the church was divinely instituted, had destroyed the church. The papacy had set itself up in the place of Christ and had annihilated faith and church; instead of the Word of God, human ordinances were governing the papal church. Its very foundation had to be destroyed and the dominance of the gospel had to be restored. When Luther burned the canon law books and the papal bull at the Elster Gate in December, 1520, he gave a signal noted far and wide; he maintained his conclusion until the end of his life, demonstrating it once again in 1545 with the writing of *Against the Papacy at Rome, Established by the Devil.*[50] This did not prevent him from expressing kind words about individual popes, however, in contrast to the medieval attitiude which personified the Antichrist in the form of individual popes and left the papal institution itself unscathed.[51]

At the beginning of January, 1521, Luther was finally excommunicated and in May, 1521, the Diet of Worms also

placed him under the temporal ban—and not only Luther,
but all his followers, all who supported him, and all who
printed, sold, or read his writings.[52] When that happened,
the fugitive had already been brought by Frederick the
Wise to the safety of the Wartburg and was out of reach.
But the Edict of Worms also had little power because in
no way did it—even though it purported to—reflect the
unanimous will of the emperor and all the estates. It did
indeed express the emperor's will. The hopes which Luther
and the Evangelicals nourished for years about the "young
noble blood" of Charles V were crassly opposed to the
emperor's real will. From beginning to end of his reign
he saw himself as the protector and governor of the Roman
church, but political circumstances prevented the emperor
from actually doing anything. The premature departure
from the Diet of Worms by the French ambassador (and
also by Frederick the Wise) cast a dark shadow over the
future; before the end of the year the first war with France
broke out. Although Charles won in 1525, the struggle re-
sumed in 1526 and by 1544 a total of four wars had been
fought with France for supremacy in Europe. They forced
the emperor to refrain from taking decisive action against
Germany and its religious disputes, since he needed the
help of the estates not only against France, but also against
the continual westward march of the Turks, who captured
Rhodes in 1522 and in 1526 triumphed in Hungary. When
the emperor's brother, Archduke Ferdinand, succeeded
King Louis II of Hungary who had been killed in 1520
at the battle of Mohács, it meant only an apparent
strengthening of the imperial position. By 1529 the Turks
had reached the gates of Vienna and continued their assault
until Hungary finally became a Turkish province in 1541.

Charles V continually needed money and troops from the princes who were more and more turning to the Reformation cause.

The general political situation, even the political aspirations of the territorial rulers, and the history of the Reformation are more closely associated with each other than it sometimes appears in the church history books, which not infrequently consider and evaluate the events taking place within the church in isolation. By no means does this indicate that we should view the expansion of the Reformation and the decision of individual princes in its favor in exclusively political terms, as secular historians tend to do. They not infrequently neglect or give insufficient weight to certain aspects of the history of the Reformation—a good example of this is the discussion about the reason for Frederick the Wise's actions—and thus cut themselves off from a full understanding of the Reformation. We ought not overlook the fact that where the Reformation was introduced "from above," as happened in Albertine Saxony after the death of Duke George, the "Catholic" character of the territory had been maintained up to then only by governmental force; without it at least a large part of Ducal Saxony would long since have become Evangelical. The same thing is true of the other Catholic territories. They only stemmed the advance of the Reformation with great difficulty, and would have been conquered by the middle of the century if the preaching of the gospel had been permitted. It was only this political opposition, then the defeat of the Protestants in the Schmalkald War with the Peace of Augsburg's legitimization of compelling religious conformity, and finally the variety of methods used by the

Counter Reformation which saved Catholicism from ex-
tinction in most German territories in the sixteenth century.

Against the will of the emperor, and the pressure of the
pope and the staunchly Catholic estates (chiefly Brandenburg, Ducal Saxony, and Bavaria), the Edict of Worms
with its proscription of the Reformation remained little
more than a scrap of paper, a circumstance which is obvious
on the basis of the political situation depicted above. After
the Diet had met three times in Nuremberg between 1522
and 1524, it was intended at the first Diet of Speyer in 1526
to enforce the Edict of Worms at last, but, instead, what
resulted was a proclamation (whose provisions Archduke
Ferdinand could limit only with great pains) by almost all
the estates of their desire to reform. Even when the Catholics had a majority at the second Diet of Speyer in 1529
and an imperial message demanded the repeal of this decision made at the first Diet of Speyer, all that happened
was that the Evangelicals made a protest—in matters of
faith majority decisions are invalid, for everyone must
"conduct himself as he has to give account to God," thus
earning for themselves the term "Protestant"—and joined
together in an alliance for defensive purposes.

By that time the development of Evangelical territorial
churches was well under way. But before such a task was
undertaken, a long and difficult way had already been followed. When Luther became "Knight George" in 1521 and
was cut off at the Wartburg from participating in the events
in Wittenberg (letters, writings, and a secret visit to Wittenberg could not substitute for a constant presence), the
Reformation was faced with deciding whether and how
those things in which new insights had been attained
should be put into practice: What should be done about

the celibacy of the priests, about the monasteries, and about the worship services, especially the mass? It was clear from Luther's writings that the former practices were refuted by the gospel. People believed they were in accord with Luther's spirit when they began to act.

On August 24, 1521, Bartholomew Bernhardi, provost in Wittenberg's neighboring town of Kemberg, married; others followed him, the most prominent of them, Justus Jonas, in February, 1522. In November, 1521, 13 monks left the Augustinian monastery in Wittenberg under tumultuous circumstances, and in 1522 the council of the order permitted all to leave who so desired, and established new rules for the monastic life of those who intended to remain: They were to devote themselves to teaching the Holy Scriptures or earn their living by manual labor. In September, 1521, the Lord's Supper in both kinds was celebrated in the City Church, on October 13 the mass was discontinued in the monastery chapel, and in December a mob drove those priests who wanted to say mass out of the City Church. At Christmas, 1521, a new form of worship service was held for the entire congregation in the City Church (revised liturgy, communion in both kinds without confession preceding) and was repeated there and at other locations. After all but one of the altars were removed from the chapel of the Augustinian monastery, the monks burned the idolatrous images and a Wittenberg city ordinance required the removal of all pictures from the City Church.

Leaders in all of this were Karlstadt and Gabriel Zwilling, acting more on the basis of enthusiasm than theological arguments, assisted by three prophets from Zwickau who claimed to be immediate witnesses of God, whose Spirit spoke to them and through them to others. Soon chaos reigned supreme; each member of the clergy did whatever he pleased, although not a few of them held back from the innovations, some because of fundamental opposition. The uninstructed congregation, impressed by the spectacle and dragged along by these new events, did not know what was going on; some still clung to the old faith. The imperial authorities, at the special instigation of Duke George, forbade all innovations and demanded that the elector restore things to their original status. Finally the city council knew no other alternative than to appeal to Luther to return to Wittenberg. He came, although banned and proscribed, and expressly rejected any protection from the elector in his possible danger: "He who believes the most, can protect the most."[53] For a week he preached daily, and after that peace reigned in the congregation.[54]

Celibacy and monasteries remained abolished, along with the private masses, theologically objectionable sections were removed from the mass liturgy, but everything else which had been abolished in the Wittenberg disturbances was restored. It was then dismantled step by step: Communion in both kinds was introduced and the Catholic mass was transformed into a "German Mass" by introducing the German language into the worship service. Even the Wittenberg church ordinance of 1522 came into existence via a detour through the Leisnig *Ordinance of a Common Chest* of 1523. But the reforms were extended until 1525; before acting in the ecclesiastical sphere, one had to convince the community of the legitimacy of what one was doing. Abuses, shown to be such, would fall by themselves; this was the essence of Luther's Invocavit sermons, and he followed his own advice.

Because of this Luther has been accused of being a "conservative," and to a certain extent this is true. Quite differently than Zwingli, who went about his reform of ecclesiastical practices with cool rationality, Luther, who was rooted much more deeply in Catholicism than the Swiss reformer, only altered what needed to be changed because of theological necessity and left everything else unchanged. If a theological reason exists, Luther could—and this must be said as a corrective to the repeated claim of his conservatism—go to the most extreme and radical consequences. If and where people are true Christians, so he claimed, they need neither the state nor its laws, neither any sort of governmental body nor external rules; the law of love that rules them makes all of that superfluous.[55] In a community of real Christians there is a "third kind of order" with a totally different kind of worship service, as well as a totally different life of the entire community.[56] In all of this Luther goes far beyond the "radical" Zwingli, to whom such an "anarchistic" political program or a similar "pietistic" social order would have been an abomination.

In 1526 (at the time of the first Diet of Speyer, to remind us of the political component) the intentional construction of an Evangelical territorial church began outside Wittenberg, at first in Electoral Saxony. At Luther's suggestion, a network of visitations spread through the territory in order to stop ecclesiastical abuses and to regulate external order.[57] Both tasks were found to be extremely necessary; the results of the visitation are the *Instructions for the Visitors of Parish Pastors in Electoral Saxony,*[58] essentially written by Melanchthon, and Luther's Small and Large Catechisms. They come from 1529; in 1530 a new chapter begins in the history of the Lutheran church and in Luther's own attitude, for now the "young Luther" is gradually replaced by the "mature Luther." This change is evidenced externally by the Diet of Augsburg and the Augsburg Confession presented there, and foreshadowed internally by the events since the year 1525.

The year 1525 itself has decisive significance. In January there appeared Luther's *Against the Heavenly Prophets in the Matter of Images and Sacraments,* directed against Karlstadt and enthusiasts represented by him. "In the name of God and our dear Lord Jesus Christ. There has been a change in the weather. I had almost relaxed and thought the matter was finished; but then it suddenly arises anew," [60] is the way Luther begins his writing, thus depicting the seriousness of the situation. It was not merely because the dispute was with Karlstadt (a long-time professor on the Wittenberg faculty and its dean when Luther earned his Doctorate of Theology and became a professor, who at least publicly had been his friend and fellow-worker), but rather because of the subject under consideration. Important enough was the issue of the Lord's Supper. Karlstadt's strange view (Christ had pointed toward himself when speaking the words of institution, so the bread and wine in the Lord's Supper could not be his body and blood) was easy enough to refute, but it was merely the beginning of the sacramentarian controversy. This controversy, at first fought by their supporters, but finally by Luther and Zwingli themselves, produced more and more vehement polemical writings until finally, after the Marburg Colloquy of 1529 had failed to bring unity, it divided the Reformation and "Lutheran" and "Reformed" became separated from one another by a deep gulf. Calvin's attempt to bridge it failed and resulted in even more bitter disputes in the so-called Westphal controversy. Not until our own generation has even a first step toward overcoming the difference been possible.

Even more significant was the question raised by Karlstadt and the enthusiasts about the Old Testament's validity for the Christian. Images were prohibited in the Old Testament; did this prohibition and all its consequences have to be adopted by the Reformation? By itself this would not have been decisive (in Switzerland, for example, images were prohibited), but much more than this stood behind the issue of images. Those who contended for a prohibition of the images proceeded on the basis of the total and literal validity of the Old Testament for the Christian with all the consequences of that position, especially the use of the sword against the godless.

An example of a man holding this view is Thomas Müntzer who today is often unjustly understood as a social revolutionary, but whose activity can only be explained on the basis of his theological presupposition which corresponded to this sort of view of the Old Testament. Luther, on his part, answered that in the Old Testament everything depends on the person addressed, whether it is the Jews alone or all the pious: "For Moses [i.e., the Jewish ceremonial law] is given to the Jewish people alone, and does not concern us Gentiles and Christians. We have our gospel and New Testament." [61] For to the Christian applies only what is said to all the pious, i.e., not said to the Jews, as Paul states: "Christ is the end of the law." [62] Moses is the law for the Jews,[63] not for the Christians. The Old Testament should be read by all Christians, Luther nevertheless declared, for the examples it contains, for the prophesies and promises of Christ, for the "beautiful examples of faith, of love, and of the cross" among the patriarchs, and so that "we should learn to trust in God and love him." [64]

In Karlstadt one also finds mysticism as an additional source of revelation, an idea which then plays a great role in the "left wing" of the Reformation. It is the sinking into one's self and obeying the voice of God which one most loudly hears in the common man. Luther emphatically opposed such an idea. No sooner had this controversy broken out than it was eclipsed by the Peasants' War. In the summer of 1524 the peasants in the Black Forest revolted. By the beginning of 1525 the revolt had reached Upper Swabia and spread farther until it finally extended into central Germany. At first the advance of the peasant armies seemed unchallenged, for the estates were insufficiently armed and helpless in the face of the revolt.

It is correct that the peasants appealed to the gospel in writings such as the *Twelve Articles of the Peasants in Swabia,* and based their demands for freedom from serfdom and all its onerous duties on Luther's *The Freedom of a Christian.* But it is obvious that in their interpretation of *The Freedom of a Christian* they had nothing at all to do with Luther. There is also no causal relationship between Luther and the outbreak or the bloody conclusion of the Peasants' War. There would have been a Peasants' War without Luther, for its preliminary stages go back to the fifteenth century, even to the fourteenth century if one includes events in England.[65] So much tinder had accumulated that it only took a tiny spark to set off a great explosion. Astrological calculations had created the general expectation that the year 1525 would experience a global catastrophe and tension was at the breaking point.

Luther, to whom the peasants had expressly appealed as arbitrator, expressed himself several times on the Peasants' War, the first time with his *Admonition to Peace, a Reply to the Twelve Articles of the Peasants in Swabia,* since in these articles the peasants had mentioned him by name and especially since they had solemnly declared in the twelfth article their willingness to retract their position if convinced by the Scriptures.[66] Nothing resulted from this writing, for by the time it was printed and achieved a limited circulation blood had long since been spilled by both sides; neither the peasants nor the princes paid any attention to the admonition to a peaceful solution. Even less can Luther be accused of responsibility for the bloody conclusion of the Peasants' War and the atrocities of the victorious princes. The accusation that in *Against the Robbing and Murdering Hordes of Peasants* Luther advocated in horrible words the slaughtering of peasants, misses the point in two ways. First, Luther did not publish a work with this title. He wrote it as a supplement for a second edition of *Admonition to Peace* (Also *Against the Murdering and Robbing Hordes of* the Other *Peasants*). Only when read together with the first writing does one get his complete meaning; it was the greed of the publishers outside Wittenberg that led to the separate printing and the altered title. And second, in both its original and its abbreviated (and thus forged) form this writing had no influence on the course of events. The supplement to the second edition of the *Admonition* was written at the beginning of May, 1525, and on May 15 the decisive battle at Frankenhausen took place. At that time there were not even copies of Luther's original writing in the hands of the combatants, not to mention the reprinting.

It was first read *after* the defeat of the peasants as the princes wreaked their bloody vengeance on the now unarmed peasants; it is from this that the persistent negative echo of this inevitably misunderstood writing comes. And, finally, if Luther is accused (as Engels does) of making a 180-degree turn in 1525 in his attitude toward armed revolt in order to save the Reformation, this completely misses the mark. Luther's attitude is consistent from the beginning. As early as 1522 he had written: "I am and always will be on the side of those against whom insurrection is directed, no matter how unjust their cause; I am opposed to those who rise in insurrection, no matter how just their cause. . . ."[67] Consequently, in 1520, when armed conflict broke out between the students and citizens in Wittenberg so that troops had to enter the city to restore order, Luther from the pulpit expressly rejected the riot, to the fervent indignation of the entire university, especially the students.[68]

There were other events of the year 1525 which provided material for contemporary polemics, and even more for polemics of later generations. On June 13, 1525, Luther married Katherina von Bora. According to medieval superstition, the Antichrist would be born of the union of an apostate monk and a renegade nun. Just to mention this should be sufficient to shed light on the situation. The Peasants' War was scarcely over, and only a week before the marriage Luther had defended himself against the attacks on his attitude concerning it.[69] That just made the step even more difficult for others to understand—now as well as then. In addition, only a few months had passed since the first thoughts of a marriage with Katie (who as recently as March was still considering Amsdorf) and the actual ceremony. This and many other apparently offensive acts can quickly be explained by the fact that Luther wanted to give a clear testimony that no one could misunderstand, especially at a time when it might appear that everything was out of joint, that the devil was "stirring the soup," and that the end of the world seemed nearer than ever.[70] Since 1521 many Evangelical theologians had already married, including Melanchthon—with Luther's encouragement—but it was not until Luther himself took this step that the Evangelical preaching against celibacy and monastic vows received its irrevokable stamp of approval. "I expect," wrote Luther a few days later, "the angels laugh and the devils weep thereat." [71] There is no hint of any sort of romance before the marriage.[72] Perhaps boredom with his "bachelor life" was significant, for Luther was then 42 years old and he lived alone with Prior Brisger in the vacant and neglected monastery without anyone to take care of them. His father's wish for the marriage of his son certainly still had a more powerful influence, [73] but both items took a back seat to the real motive.[74] This marriage, which at first had little to do with the modern concept of "love," developed into a deep, loving relationship, far superior in its sincerity to countless modern marriages.[75]

Also it was in October, 1525, that the first German worship service took place in Wittenberg, and at Christmas the *German Mass* was finally introduced. With this a decisive turning point had been reached, for simultaneously with the publication of this *German Mass,* an Enchiridion was published. This was a hymnal containing spiritual songs and psalms for the laity (the Wittenberg *Spiritual Hymn Booklet* of 1524 had been designed for choir use). With this *German Mass* reform of the worship was completed,

and this form became the norm for German Lutheran territories for centuries. This German worship service, congre-
gational hymnal, and catechism (which Luther had emphatically demanded in the *German Mass*) provided the elements for the internal development of Evangelical congregations; the visitations commencing in 1526 furnished the
external framework for the consolidation of the Evangelical territorial churches.

At the end of the eventful year of 1525 came Luther's
dispute with Erasmus and humanism, and his treatise
*Bondage of the Will*.[76] After much hesitation, Erasmus
picked up his pen and joined the ranks of Luther's opponents. In doing so he was attempting, within the clash of
different opinions of his time, to take the path of least
resistance and optimal (even *economic*) benefit. He had
once thought that everything taught by the Reformation,
whether originating in Wittenberg or in Zurich, had long
before been said by him. On the other hand, the opponents
of the Reformation accused him of being the Lutherans'
standard bearer. Both views were completely contrary to
the facts. Luther saw things much more incisively and as
early as 1516 had criticized Erasmus' shallowness.[77] With
the publication of Erasmus' *Freedom of the Will* in 1524 the
difference between the two men came out into the open.[78]
In the final analysis, said Erasmus, religion was basically
ethics. Since speculative assertion, as well as statements on
church practice, are uncertain, one must submit to those
doctrinal decisions of the church that are based on the
uniform teachings of most of the theologians, not on those
concerning which the opponents cannot agree among themselves. Since all people base their doctrine on revelation, how
can there be any guarantee of truth? Erasmus would have

preferred to be a skeptic. When difficult questions such as free will are to be discussed they should be dealt with only by the learned and then only with extreme caution, for the doctrine of the bondage of the will would give the masses only an excuse for immoral acts.

While strongly criticizing Erasmus' general position, Luther, in his answer, which along with the Large Catechism he considered among his most important writings, thanks Erasmus for what he has done for "languages and literature." He should stick to that. "But God has not yet willed or granted that you should be equal to the matter at present at issue between us." [79] Luther emphatically declared that even if there existed such a thing as free will in regard to justification—which he showed to be impossible by adducing a great number of scriptural passages—he did not want it.[80] For if salvation would depend on us, we would never be able to attain it in the face of the overwhelming power of the devil. Even if there were no devil and no danger, we, left to ourselves, would always remain uncertain. No matter how hard we might work or how much we might do,

> there would always remain an anxious doubt whether it pleased God or whether he required something more. . . . But, now, since God has taken my salvation out of my hands into his, making it depend on his choice and not mine, and has promised to save me, not by my own work or exertion but by his grace and mercy, I am assured and certain both that he is faithful and will not lie to me, and also that he is too great and powerful for any demons or any adversities to be able to break him or to snatch me from him.[81]

The same sort of dissociation that took place with the humanists occurred during the next years with the Swiss and South German theologians. In 1520 Luther had taught the real presence of Christ in the Lord's Supper without precisely defining the way in which it came to be, although he emphatically denied the Catholic doctrine of transubstantiation. Zwingli held a similar view, but both parties continued to develop their original positions. Zwingli, after adopting Hoen's interpretation that the *est* in the words of institution really means *significat,* felt free to view the Lord's Supper as an act of remembrance and thanksgiving for Christ's sacrificial death by the congregation which had already been justified through faith. Such an act had the character of a confession and an obligation, and the real presence of Christ was not only unnecessary, but also impossible because Christ has been seated at the right hand of God ever since his ascension (Karlstadt's old argument). Aided by the doctrine of Christ's ubiquity (omnipresence), Luther developed his concept of the real presence in more and more realistic terms; whoever did not accept the *est* together with all its consequences, even to the *manducatio impiorum* ("oral reception by the wicked"), did not belong to the church of Christ. Despite all the efforts of Landgrave Philip of Hesse, it was no surprise that the attempt to reach agreement on this matter failed at the Marburg Colloquy (October 1-4, 1529).

In the year 1530, as in 1526, a new episode began in the history of the Reformation. The Diet of Augsburg in 1530 marks the external turning point. The emperor, who had concluded a peace with France in 1529, intended the diet to solve the religious question, i.e., to crush the Reformation. Charles V declared that the Augsburg Confession (written by Melanchthon, but whose first part was derived from Luther's Schwabach Articles) presented there by the Evangelicals had been refuted by the Confutation prepared by the Catholics, despite Melanchthon's Apology. The diet's decision renewed the Edict of Worms, ordered the restitution of all expropriated ecclesiastical property under penalty of the ban, and commanded that under penalty of death no one should be prevented from attending mass and adhering to the old faith. In the face of this situation most of the evangelical estates organized the Smalcald League at the end of 1530 and Luther issued his sharpest writing yet, *Dr. Martin Luther's Warning to His Dear German People,*[82] releasing people from obedience to the emperor [83] and predicting war or insurrection.[84]

Neither prediction came to pass, for the danger posed by the Turks forced the emperor to be amenable to the Evangelicals whose support he needed. The Diet of Regensburg in 1532 and the so-called Peace of Nuremberg of July 23, 1532, provided that religious arguments would come to a standstill and there would be no armed conflict before a general church council could meet. Nevertheless, for the first time the shadow of what was to come had fallen over the Evangelical estates. The Reformation won some glittering external victories in the next few years. In 1534 Ulrich of Württemberg was restored to power under Philip of Hesse's leadership and the territory became Evangelical; in the same year the Reformation was introduced in Anhalt and Pomerania; Nassau, Mecklenburg, Pfalz-Neuburg, Brunswick, and numerous cities followed suit, and in 1539 the main bastions of Catholicism in central Germany, Brandenburg and Ducal Saxony, also fell. Even in the ecclesiastical territories the Evangelical populace was success-

ful. In Magdeburg and Halberstadt the citizens obtained
the right to introduce the Reformation from Albrecht of
Mainz—through payment of an indemnity. Even with the
archbishop of Cologne and the bishop of Münster and
Osnabrück there were leanings toward the new faith, or
at least toleration of it, and things were similar in other
areas. The Smalcald League reached the height of its influence and its range extended far beyond the German
borders.

Yet this Protestantism had something restrictive about it.
It is true that it finally consolidated itself after 1530, after
the initial steps were taken in 1526. But at the same time
it took certain characteristics which remind one of Lutheranism in the age of orthodoxy after Luther's death. Luther
himself gradually was transformed from the "prophet" of
the earlier years into the "church father." An openness in
Lutheranism seemed to be indicated by the Wittenberg
Concord of 1536,[85] but everything else showed an increasing stabilization that one might really call a narrowing. All
one needs to do to see this clearly is to examine the different
treatment of any theme in Luther's writings from the beginning of the 1520s and those from the period after 1530.
For example, one might compare the changes in his
prefaces to the Bible, or look at the difference between his
*Infiltrating and Clandestine Preachers* [86] of 1532 and those
writings on matters of church organization in the 1520s,
or any other topic of one's choice. One cannot treat any
theme about Luther, not even the central one of the Scriptures, by simply collecting and systematically arranging
his statements on a subject without regard to the time
and occasion of their writing. It is necessary, if one wants
to obtain results that will stand the test of time, to pay

close attention to the development from the "young" to the "mature" Luther. If one puts all the utterances of Luther, from the early lectures to the last ones on Genesis, on the same plane—as people are still doing—one may be able to preserve a "leveled off" Luther, but never the real, living Luther.

If one wonders about Luther's main activity during these years (and before), it is without doubt the exposition of the Scriptures, both in the classroom *and* in the pulpit. All his life Luther limited himself to the task of the professorship *in biblia* which was assigned him in 1512; he also preached frequently in the City Church as a substitute for the pastor Johannes Bugenhagen. Both tasks—teaching and preaching—must be seen as a unit. This sort of exposition of Scripture made use of all the tools available, but was much more than present-day exegesis, since it included all dogmatic questions and provided answers for pastoral practice in the church, even when it dealt with texts which seemed unsuitable for such a purpose. For instance, during the last ten years of his life, 1535-1545, Luther lectured only on the book of Genesis. Among the modern theological disciplines, church history is the only one missing in his endeavors; it is found only on the periphery and then only for the purpose of providing illustrations and facts for the polemical task. His exposition of Scripture is flanked by writings of topical interest. When one inquires about the central theme, it is without doubt the proper relation of law and gospel, in which everything is included and out of which come the answers to all questions, even those concerning the state and many other topics.[87]

All in all, Luther's writings from the mid-1530s on decrease both in number and in size. Noteworthy is the fact that among them are four writings directed against the Jews, with no less than three of them coming from the single year 1543.[88] In his early days Luther took a firm stand against the contemporary mistreatment of Jews and advocated a new relationship with them in *That Jesus Christ Was Born a Jew* (1523),[89] but late in life he directed such sharp words against them that modern anti-Semites, such as Julius Streicher at the Nuremberg Tribunal, have cited them in an attempt at self-justification. This overlooks the decisive difference: Luther wrote out of his disappointment that the Jews had not let themselves be converted to Christianity, but in spite of all attempts at conversion had hardened their hearts in animosity to it. It was solely because of the opposition of faith; any "ethnic" opposition was totally irrelevant for Luther. For him a baptized Jew was a dear brother. Further, in contrast to the measures which he recommended for the stiffnecked Jews, Luther demanded of the pastors and congregations only that they refrain from associating with Jews (anything more than this was expressly excluded),[90] so that they might not be strengthened in their opposition to Christianity: "We cannot help it if they do not share our belief. It is impossible to force anyone to believe."[91]

This would be the "reactionary" Luther. But there is also a "progressive" Luther. As early as 1519 he had written against "usury," i.e., the financial and commercial activities of his time, and had frequently repeated his opposition until he wrote *To the Pastors, That They Should Preach Against Usury* in 1540.[92] In an appendix to *To the Christian Nobility* of 1520, which dealt with the "failings of the clergy"[93] which should be corrected at a council, he spoke not only about charging interest, but also about the trading companies of the Fuggers and others, and raged at the world-wide "monopolistic capitalism," repeating his attacks up to the last years of his life. There is much that remains to be said about this "up-to-date" Luther, so contemporary about things beyond the church and congregation. Unfortunately, however, his influence on the contemporary scene has decreased, even in church circles, because his writings have been considered of the past and not of the present. People have been too concerned about the "historical dust" that has been superseded by later developments, rather than what is of timeless validity in his writings. A great deal of loss in substance, especially in the Lutheran church, can be explained in this way.

When Luther died on February 18, 1546, at the age of 63—after painstakingly achieving a reconciliation between the feuding counts of Mansfeld, the rulers of his ancestral home—his work was externally still unendangered. But the thunderclouds of the Smalcald War, which was to bring German Protestantism into extreme danger, already threatened on the horizon; incomprehensively its approach was unnoticed by the Evangelicals. With masterful political moves, and assisted by the shortsightedness and weakness of some princes, the emperor managed to outmaneuver the Evangelical estates in the years after 1540. The war which broke out on July 20, 1546, brought them complete defeat and even deep personal humiliation to its leaders.

At the "Ironclad Diet" in Augsburg in 1548 the way seemed clear for the triumphant emperor to accomplish his dual goal of restoring the religious unity of the empire and the central authority of the emperor, but he had incorrectly evaluated the inner power of the Evangelical faith and the strength of the territorial princes. The imperial "Interim" [94] had no hope of acceptance by congregations and pastors; the resistance of the estates masterfully led by Maurice of Saxony gained more support, until Maurice finally outmaneuvered the emperor just as Charles had earlier done to the Evangelicals. The Peace of Augsburg of 1555 was the final result of the long, tenaciously fought struggle.[95] Its provisions—later summarized in the phrase *cuius regio, eius religio*—state that the decision concerning the faith of a territory's citizens was in the hand of that territory's government (except for the imperial free cities and, according to the Declaration of Ferdinand, the Evangelical areas in the ecclesiastical territories). This is a complete caricature of what Luther wanted, for he recognized that a decision about faith could be made only by an individual. Yet the fact must not be overlooked that this was the first time that another confession had been recognized in imperial law and guaranteed an existence. The pope's bitter rejection of this peace and the repeated attempts by every means to annul this confessional parity—which lasted until the Thirty Years' War—availed nothing. The unified world of the Middle Ages had been demolished; a new world had taken its place.

But where do Luther and the Reformation belong in this context—in the Middle Ages or the modern world? Philosophers, such as Nietzsche, and historians, such as Troeltsch, have often seen Luther as a medieval man; the question is frequently answered with a statement by Conrad Ferdinand Meyer: "His spirit is a battleground of two ages." [96] Certainly many medieval elements can be traced in Luther's thought. But when one looks at his work and primarily the effects of his work, one can unmistakably date the beginning of the modern age with Luther and the Reformation.

The "Copernican turning point" began with the posting of the theses on October 31, 1517—not in the action itself nor the motive behind it, but in its results. What one now calls "plurality" began to assert itself at that time; with the Peace of Augsburg in 1555 it won governmental and legal recognition with all the incalculable consequences. Even those schools of thought that today regard Luther as a monster or at best a fossil are his heirs; without him and the Reformation breakthrough our modern world of thought would not have developed as it did.

The direct influence of Luther on the intellectual life of the modern age has not yet been examined as thoroughly as it deserves, but the material that already exists shows his vast importance, even in places where one might not at first expect to find it. One would not ordinarily connect Luther with the modern demand for tolerance; yet its forerunner Sebastian Castellio, in his famous work *Concerning the Persecution of Heretics,* numbered Luther among his chief witnesses.[97] Here, too, things become clearer when one looks more closely. Much greater and more significant than what is already visible are the invisible, hidden effects of Luther which still continue. The summary judgment must be that the intellectual life of the modern world would never have come into existence without Martin Luther and the Reformation.

# Philip Melanchthon

Philip Melanchthon was born in Bretten on February 16, 1497, to the electoral armorer Georg Schwarzert (in humanistic fashion Philip altered his surname to its Greek form) and his wife Barbara Reuter. From 1508 (the year of his father's untimely death) until 1509 Melanchthon, who previously had been instructed privately, was enrolled in the Latin school in Pforzheim and in 1509, at the age of 12, matriculated at the university in Heidelberg. At the age of 14 he earned the Bachelor of Arts there and at 16 obtained the Master of Arts in Tübingen.

In 1518 the 21-year-old was called, on the recommendation of his great-uncle Reuchlin, to be professor of Greek at the university in Wittenberg. Here the humanist developed into a close follower of Luther and energetic co-worker for the Reformation. His Loci communes signal the high point of this period. The Wittenberg disturbances during 1521-1522, in which during Luther's absence he found himself for the first time in the role of the one primarily responsible for

*the Reformation movement, demanded so much of
him that his teaching responsibility had to be reduced. All of Luther's attempts to draw him entirely
into the theological faculty were resisted by Melanchthon (who never progressed beyond the degree of
Bachelor of Theology), and he now devoted himself
again primarily to his area of philology and history.
Yet during the succeeding years he retained a leading
role, second only to his close friend Luther, in the
Reformation that proceeded from Wittenberg.*

*His incomparable gift for systematic formulation and
clear, understandable presentation, which he had already displayed in the* Loci *communes, was put to
good use once again at the Diet of Augsburg in writing
the Augsburg Confession and even more (because of
the unfavorable circumstances) in writing the Apology
which defended and supplemented it. This outstanding
thinker and theologian was at the same time a hesi-
tant and weak person; thus the position which he took
at the negotiations in Augsburg met with considerable
criticism. In addition, his theological development concerning the Lord's Supper (in 1540 he published an
altered version of the Augsburg Confession) led him
away from his original position (in 1536 his disputes
with Cordatus began), and it was mirrored in several
reworkings of his* Loci *(new editions were published in
1535, 1543-1544, and 1559).*

*In the stormy years following Luther's death,
Melanchthon could not maintain the position as Luther's successor that rightly was his. His human weakness and increasing theological alienation from the
hardening position of Lutheranism involved him in
continuing bitter controversies with the so-called Gnesio-
lutherans and led him more and more to become the*

*head of the school of "Philipists." On April 19, 1560,*
*death released Melanchthon from the "rage of the*
*theologians" at whose hands he had suffered much.*
*The significance and accomplishment of the "Pre-*
*ceptor of Germany," as he was soon called by his*
*thankful students, extends far beyond the field of*
*theology, and the system of Protestant schools and uni-*
*versities owes much to him.*

~~~~~~~~~~~~~~~~~~~~~~~~~~~~~~~~~~~~~~~~~~

When we speak about the Reformers today, even the
theologians—not to mention the laity—generally think of
Luther and Calvin (the latter only because the plural
requires it); if we speak about *the* Reformer, it is Luther
who is meant. Even Calvin takes a back seat in relation to
him, and as a rule Zwingli and Melanchthon are completely forgotten—the former is seen as only a preliminary
herald of Calvin and the latter has virtually disappeared in
Luther's shadow. This does not to justice to the historical
reality. (We shall speak of this again in the Postscript.)[1]

That Melanchthon has been almost completely forgotten
is more than an injustice. During the last quarter of his
life he was indeed on the receiving end of vehement attacks
by those who appeared as Luther's true heirs—and not
without some justification. But even in 1580 when the
German Lutheran church really came into existence
through the acceptance of the Book of Concord, the con-
fessionally conscious Lutherans of that day (who were always prepared to fight against all doctrinal deviation) never
considered repudiating Melanchthon. *Concordia: Christian,*
*Reiterated, and Unanimous Confession of the Doctrine and*
*Faith of the undersigned Electors, Princes, and Estates who*

*Embrace the Augsburg Confession and of their Theologians* was the title of Lutheranism's Magna Carta in which the confessions of the Reformation and of the ancient church were collected with the Formula of Concord to form a doctrinal foundation. In its preface Melanchthon and his writings were expressly cited: "Nor do we want to have rejected or condemned any other profitable writings of Master Philip Melanchthon . . . ," although with good reason they added, "in so far as they are in agreement with the norm incorporated in the [Formula of] Concord." [2] The only reason they spoke this way was that reference to the Altered Augsburg Confession of 1540 could not be avoided. Concerning it, they stated that "we never understood or accepted the second edition in any other sense than that of the first Augsburg Confession [i.e., the one in 1530] as it was submitted." [3] All that was condemned were the false teachers who "attempted to hide their error" behind the edition of 1540. [4]

It is only in this roundabout way that Melanchthon's authorship of the Augsburg Confession is even mentioned. In fact, it was already thought of as leading an existence of its own apart from its author—as did the Apology and the Treatise on the Power and Primacy of the Pope, which were both also written by Melanchthon—and this thinking continued to mount until people completely forgot that every one of the officially adopted confessional writings of the Reformation came from Melanchthon's pen. In addition to these three writings of Melanchthon just mentioned, the Book of Concord contains Martin Luther's Smalcald Articles and his Small Catechism and Large Catechism, so it would appear—if one merely counts the writings and the pages—that Luther is equally represented alongside Melanchthon. In fact, however, the two catechisms were never expressly adopted as confessions, either by the estates or the theologians, but quietly attained this status by virtue of their contents and use. And even the Smalcald Articles, although prepared for consideration at the meeting of the Smalcald League in 1537, were never officially signed by the estates as a confession. It was the influence of Melanchthon that convinced the princes that such an action would be superfluous in view of the existence of the Augsburg Confession and the Apology. He probably considered the language of the Smalcald Articles too cutting and Luther was extremely ill at the time and could exercise no influence on the deliberations. Nevertheless, the theologians assembled at Smalcald, at Bugenhagen's instigation, signed the articles at the close of the meeting as an expression of their personal convictions. Thus the Smalcald Articles in this circuitous fashion became a confessional document; even Melanchthon could not withhold his signature, although he subscribed with reservations concerning the article on the papacy.

This sort of thing was characteristic of Melanchthon—and we shall deal with it later—but it does not change the fact that the principal confessions of Lutheranism, the Augsburg Confession and its Apology, come from Melanchthon. The first part of the Augsburg Confession (Arts. 1-21: "Articles of Faith and Doctrine") [5] does indeed go back to Luther's so-called Schwabach Articles of 1529, but if one compares them with the final text of the Augsburg Confession it is clear just how great was Melanchthon's contribution to this first part of the Augsburg Confession. Here in an imperishable manner the content of the Evangelical faith is expressed with unexcelled clarity in classical formulations, which can be seen most clearly in the Latin text. The second part of the Augsburg Confession (Arts. 22-28: "Articles about Matters in Dispute, in which an Account is Given of the Abuses which Have Been Corrected") [6] goes back even in its earliest drafts completely to Melanchthon.

Thus Melanchthon has continued to be alive and active in Lutheranism of all times and even beyond the Lutheran church, for the 1540 version of the Augsburg Confession had a decisive significance for the Reformed church, at least in the sixteenth century. That his existence was largely anonymous was due to the magnitude of the accomplishment (as has often happened in the history of the human spirit), but it was also because of Melanchthon's repeated failure in conflict situations. Virtually every time the decisive moment came to assert a fundamental insight in a difficult situation on his own authority, Melanchthon failed. That was the case during the disturbances in Wittenberg in 1521-1522, and again in 1530 at the Diet of Augsburg in the negotiations following the presentation of the Confession, and also in the religious colloquies preceding the Smalcald War. Especially crass—and quite visible to everyone—was Melanchthon's failure following the unfortunate close of that war in the situation created by the Interim and the disputes that raged about it. It was here that Melanchthon finally lost his position as the leader of the German Reformation after Luther's death, a position that rightly should have been his because of his theoretical and practical accomplishments and of his work in complementing Luther in directing the church during the latter's lifetime.

Melanchthon's non-assertiveness and human weakness continually cast a shadow over his memory and finally reduced him to the head of what was first an influential, but then strongly attacked theological school. Of course,

Melanchthon is not the only person to have his intellectual greatness diminished by human weakness. This was true for many humanists in the sixteenth century, especially for Erasmus, the greatest of them all. The development of intellect at the expense of character is a timeless event which is continually being repeated, at least in Germany. In normal times it fortunately becomes noticeable only to a limited circle, and only becomes publicly visible in extreme and burdensome circumstances. Sufficient examples could be mentioned, but theologians only need to be reminded of the period of the church struggle during the Third Reich.

In the sixteenth century one's academic training began earlier than it does today. Nevertheless, Melanchthon was something of a prodigy. In 1509 at the age of 12 he enrolled at the University of Heidelberg, at 14 he had earned the Bachelor of Arts, and when not yet 17 he had become a Master, i.e., a university teacher. The second degree he earned at Tübingen. It is said that he left Heidelberg because they would not permit him to take the examination because of his youth.[7] Probably, however, he left because the place was too confining and the academic atmosphere too suffocating. Exactly the same thing happened to him in Tübingen. He had already learned everything there was to learn there, and he felt himself imprisoned in an academic cage; when he—21-years-old—was called as professor of Greek to Wittenberg, it was a liberation for him. His great-uncle Reuchlin played the decisive role here; it was his urgent recommendation that won the position for Melanchthon over the leading candidate of the court (and of Luther), the Leipzig professor Mosellanus.[8]

Melanchthon's literary output was already considerable. At the age of 17 he prepared a new edition of a textbook,

*Dialogus mythologicus* (1514), which later went through numerous editions.[9] In 1516 he published a Latin grammar and in 1518 a Greek grammar,[10] which appeared in 18 editions until Melanchthon gave up the responsibility for it in 1544. In 1516 he published an edition of the comedies of Terence,[11] in 1517 a translation of a tract by Plutarch,[12] and in 1518 one by Lucian.[13] The edition of Terence was especially successful, over 20 reprintings appearing during the next hundred years, but the other publications also had considerable effect, especially their prefaces[14] in which Melanchthon proclaimed his goals and ideals, as he had done in his address *On the Liberal Arts.*[15]

Almost as important as these was the fact that the edition of the *Letters of Obscure Men,* which was published in 1514 in connection with the Reuchlin controversy, contained a preface by Melanchthon.[16] This signified to the educated world the importance that Reuchlin ascribed to his grand-nephew. Erasmus as early as 1515 in his *Annotations on the New Testament* found high words of praise for this "youngster, who is scarcely more than a boy,"[17] and at the same time sent him an invitation to England.

Melanchthon went to the University of Wittenberg in 1518 as a humanist, i.e., principally a teacher of the ancient languages and expositor of the wisdom contained in them. But the areas of his interest, work, and teaching went far beyond this and included history, geography, mathematics, astronomy, and even medicine, at least in the way the ancients treated medicine. He had certainly also engaged in theological studies, but had not, at least in any obvious way, taken part in the sort of religious renewal of humanity which Erasmus was promoting, let alone in the controversies which had been raging around his new university for almost a year. It is questionable how much he knew about them when his great-uncle Reuchlin solemnly sent him off with the Old Testament words of God's blessing of Abraham.[18]

His inaugural address at the Wittenberg university on August 29, 1518, on *The Reform of University Studies*[19] still emerged totally from the humanistic presuppositions but met the local situation, where a beginning of reform in the course of studies already had been in process for several years, especially at Luther's insistence. A letter of Luther to Spalatin, written two days later, gives us a picture of the impression Melanchthon had made on his hearers. "We very quickly turned our minds and eyes from his appearance and person to the man himself,"[20] wrote Luther, referring to the unimpressive appearance of the unsightly "little man"[21] who stepped before the assembly. "We congratulate ourselves on having this man and marvel at what he has in him." Melanchthon "delivered an extremely learned and absolutely faultless address. All esteemed and admired him greatly...." That Melanchthon had captured the hearts of the students is proved by the way they flocked to his lectures; Spalatin reported 400 in December, 1518,[22] and 600 at the end of 1520, while at the same time Luther had barely 400 in his class.[23]

In the letter just mentioned Luther had pledged Spalatin, who was the official at the court of the elector of Saxony responsible for the university, to do everything possible for Melanchthon's external welfare, so that he might not be enticed away from Wittenberg by a better offer from another university. Two days later he reminded Spalatin of this obligation and added: "He especially makes all theologians zealous to study Greek—the most outstanding ones, as well as the average and the weak." [24]

"For if he stays well [and does not ruin his health through excessive zeal for academic work], I do not know from whom we may expect greater things," wrote Luther to Erasmus on March 28, 1519.[25] In his first letter directly to Melanchthon, written from Augsburg on October 11, 1518, Luther already addressed him as "my dearest Philip." [26] He would rather die than recant, declares Luther, even though that would mean the most difficult thing he would have to suffer would be the loss of being eternally without the "sweetest society" with Melanchthon. In his second extant letter to Melanchthon on November 22, 1518, which, by the way, Luther signed himself "Your little brother, Martin *Eleutherius*" [this word written in Greek letters] [27] (a humorous reference both to the hearing at Augsburg and the intensified study of Greek to which he had been led by Melanchthon), the tone of personal affection is even deeper.

On his part, Melanchthon had already honored Luther in September, 1518, with a Greek poem [28] which he included in the printed form of his Wittenberg inaugural address, [29] praising Luther as the "anointed one of Israel" who is more pious than the one offering his thanks, as the "chosen servant of the indestructible truth," as the "pure leader of pious souls," as the "longed-for man, illuminated by God to be the messenger of wisdom and eternal righteousness," as the "blessed proclaimer of the divine Word and the life-giving Spirit," and similar statements.

Even though one must allow a great deal for the humanistic dedication, the fact remains that dedicating such a work to a man who had been so fiercely attacked in public meant a considerable personal risk which humanists generally took pains to avoid. It is characteristic, for example, that Reuchlin immediately sought to recall Melanchthon from what appeared to him a dangerous spot in Wittenberg, and broke off his relationship with him when he refused to leave. Luther, however, was far removed from the exaggerations of the humanists; what he displayed in these first letters was the beginning of an affection and a friendship that, despite all difficulties, endured for Luther's lifetime. He did indeed warn Melanchthon in 1518: "Play the man" (and added soothingly, "as you do") [30]—a warning that Melanchthon frequently needed in subsequent years— but again and again Luther intervened on behalf of the embattled Melanchthon, or simply ignored the attacks, so that his contemporaries not infrequently questioned whether Luther failed to grasp or did not want to grasp the magnitude and seriousness of the controversies. Melanchthon, on the other hand, often feared that Luther was angry with him and sometimes even thought that his position in Wittenberg was in danger.

In reviewing his life [31] Luther expressed the opinion that Melanchthon had been called to Wittenberg "doubtless so that I should have an associate in the work of theology," [32] for God had chosen him to be his special instrument. Melanchthon did in fact devote himself to a certain extent to theology and developed into a sort of fellow-fighter with Luther, a turn of events which no one would have expected; the words in praise of Luther cited above are only external evidence that Melanchthon had been thoroughly captivated by the Reformation theology. His letter to Oecolampadius about the Leipzig Debate, written immediately after the disputation and put into print by Melanchthon at the same time, made a sensational impression with its partisanship.[33]

Eck, whom he had sharply criticized in it, published an excited response,[34] for Melanchthon's answer had frightened him.[35] That was in the year 1519. In 1520 a writing appeared by the Dominican Tommaso Rhadino against Luther, defending and giving the theological rationale of the bull threatening excommunication.[36] At Eck's instigation it was reprinted in Germany with a different title.[37] In Wittenberg it was believed that its author was Emser, who next to Eck was a leading opponent of the Reformation, and therefore a refutation was deemed necessary. Melanchthon undertook the task, although under a pseudonym.[38] Although it was obvious enough,[39] some thought that Erasmus was the author, because of the brilliant language and rhetoric. The effectiveness of its contents is seen in the fact that two Catholic attacks on it immediately appeared.[40] When the Sorbonne in April, 1521, finally provided the opinion on Luther's cause which had been requested in 1519, and condemned 104 of Luther's statements,[41] Melanchthon again seized his pen in defense of the Reformation. Even the title shows the vehemence with which Melanchthon took the field against the Sorbonne, the most renowned university of the western world: *Against the Furious Decree of the Parisian Theologasters, an Apology by Philip Melanchthon for Luther*.[42]

As an advocate for the issue of Luther and the Reformation, Melanchthon quickly attained a leading position. Even Eck, who had wanted to discredit him as a "grammarian," not capable of dealing with theological questions, had to rethink his opinion. For very soon after he moved to Wittenberg in 1518 Melanchthon became a different per-

son. The depth of this transformation is seen in his relationship to Aristotle. In 1518 he had presented a plan to
publish a massive edition of Aristotle's writings in their
original Greek, in order to provide a new basis for academic work. But in 1521 he wrote to the theologians of
Paris: "If one Aristotle is enough to solve all the church's
errors, why do you not abolish the Holy Scriptures; why
do we not pray to Aristotle instead of Christ?"[43]

When Melanchthon engaged in the required disputation
for the degree of Bachelor of the Bible on September 19,
1519, he prepared a series of theses[44] which surprised even
Luther with their audacity.[45] Here, for example, in plain
words he stated that articles of faith which are not proved
by Scripture are void (Thesis 16), that the authority of
councils stands under Scripture (Thesis 17), and that
doubting the Catholic doctrine of the sacraments, especially
transubstantiation, is not heresy (Thesis 18). Luther was
completely overcome by Melanchthon's elaboration during
the disputation. To Staupitz he wrote:

> His answers are miracles. If Christ deign, Melanch-
> thon will make many Luthers and a most powerful
> enemy of scholastic theology, for he knows both their
> folly and Christ's rock; therefore he shall be mighty.
> Amen.[46]

As early as the summer semester of 1519 Melanchthon
began his lectures on Romans, and in 1520-1521 he repeated
them.[47] By this time Pauline theology had become for him
the center of faith and knowledge. "From no one's writings,
from no one's commentaries can one recognize Christ and
the summary of our salvation, even approximately as well
as in the letters of Paul," he declared in a festival address

to the university on January 25, 1520.[48] Out of these lectures, first intended as a summary of the most important teachings in Romans, grew Melanchthon's *Loci communes,* his "fundamental concepts of theology."[49] For throughout his life Melanchthon continued to work on the *Loci,* just as Calvin labored on his *Institutes,*[50] so that they eventually developed into the first Evangelical dogmatics textbook.[51] But in the first edition of 1521[52] Melanchthon had acquired the same inner attitude as he already possessed outwardly in defending the Reformation. At the beginning of his book against Erasmus, *The Bondage of the Will,* Luther declared that Melanchthon's *Loci* deserved "not only to be immortalized but even canonized," an indication of the sort of influence this writing had.[53] Erasmus' position had been so "beaten down and completely pulverized" by Melanchthon's *Loci,* "an unanswerable book," that Luther said he "felt profoundly sorry" for Erasmus.[54]

When one also considers that Melanchthon had made at least a significant contribution to the editorial work on Luther's commentary on Galatians,[55] which appeared in 1519, it appears that the humanist Melanchthon of 1518 had completely become a theologian. The list of his classes during these years is also evidence of this. One theological lecture followed another:

1518—Titus
1519—Psalms, Romans, Matthew
1520—Romans, Matthew
1521—Romans, 1 Corinthians, Colossians, 2 Corinthians
1522—John, Genesis
1523—John

In addition Melanchthon naturally lectured on Plutarch

(1519), Homer (1518, 1519, 1522), Pliny (1520), Lucian
(1521), Aratus (1522), Hesiod (1522), and on dialectic and
rhetoric (1521), but these lectures in his primary area of
competence were a minority compared to the theological
ones.[56]

Thus it is understandable that Luther attempted to draw
Melanchthon exclusively into the theological faculty, where
he had already become a member by earning the Bachelor
of Theology degree. As early as July 4, 1522, he had written
Spalatin:

> How I wish that you would finally see that Philip is
> relieved of the lectures on grammar, so that he might
> be free for theological ones. For it is completely unfair
> (as I have already written) that he earns a hundred
> gulden for teaching grammar, when he could instead
> be giving theological lectures of immeasurable value.
> We have more than enough teachers who can teach
> grammar just as well as Philip and must be idle be-
> cause of him.[57]

In March 1524 he renewed this proposal with the elector
himself.[58] The entire university "deeply" desired that
Melanchthon should devote himself entirely to exegetical
lectures. But he had so far refused to comply with the demand, explaining that he had been called by the elector to
deliver the "Greek lectures" and in view of that could not
accede to these requests. Luther, therefore, asked the elector
to alter Melanchthon's call accordingly. Even if his salary
would then need to be increased, "he should and must
come." Soon the appropriate order was issued by Frederick
the Wise.[59] But Melanchthon still resisted, not merely pro
forma, but quite emphatically, even though his theological
lectures were the high point of his activity (they were al-

ways filled to overflowing, but in the philosophical lectures he had only modest numbers of students and often had difficulty in holding his listeners until the end of the semester). When a salary increase of 100 gulden for Melanchthon was approved by the elector on the condition that he offer an additional theological lecture, he refused to accept the money. The work would be too taxing for him.[60]

Such an argument was only an excuse. At that time Melanchthon had consciously and emphatically devoted his work to the philosophical faculty and methodically neglected theology, for until Luther's death in 1546 he lectured only on Proverbs (1527), Romans (seven times: 1529, 1532, 1535, 1536, 1539, 1544, 1546), Colossians (1535-1536), the *Loci communes* (1542), and the theological writings of Camerarius (1545). That is all, except for one series on Colossians which cannot be dated exactly (before 1527) and a few other uncertain ones. Alongside these 12 theological lectures are about 70 non-theological ones. Not until after Luther's death in 1546 does the picture change; from then on theology once again assumes center stage.

In Melanchthon's relation to theology a break takes place, not in 1524, but as early as 1522. While Luther was suggesting to Spalatin that he should be totally drawn over to theology, Melanchthon was telling Spalatin that this was not for him. His argument is revealing: He had heard that Luther was demanding that the Greek professorship should be given to someone else; *"quod nolim"* [by no means], was Melanchthon's meager reply to that. Because it was the practice to give theological lectures after one attained the theological baccalaureate, he had done so, but he preferred to be free of this obligation.[61] This was an absolute contradiction to what Melanchthon had done ever since September, 1519, when he earned the theological degree, and what he had declared in his writings (cf. above, pp. 65-67) and letters.

What was the reason for this behavior? The explanation doubtless lies in the disturbances in Wittenberg during Luther's absence at the Wartburg from May, 1521, until March, 1522. As soon as he came to Wittenberg the current of the Reformation had forcefully swept him along and he had enthusiastically become its follower, even its standard bearer. The years 1521-1522 of the Wittenberg movement appeared to be the high point, but Melanchthon was not equal to the task of meeting the new spirits and the leadership role thrust upon him against his wishes. He let things take their own course, and was at least partially overwhelmed by the new elements; at least to some extent he was open to the "Spirit theology" of the Zwickau prophets. Luther's return from the Wartburg brought clarity to what had become a virtually impossible situation. The spiritualistic solution of Karlstadt and the enthusiasts was rejected, but through this an inner split was added to the external danger faced by the Reformation.

A certain disillusionment and insecurity overtook Melanchthon during these years. The current had pulled him far away from the old banks. Now he looked back, not with a feeling of regret, but yet endeavoring to get solid ground beneath his feet once again.[62] Luther's desire that he might give up classical philology and transfer completely to the theological faculty came in the moment of this disillusionment. Before 1522 he might have agreed to his friend's demand, but now he could only decline, because he felt incapable of the responsibility of lecturing in theology. Luther's influence over him was naturally still strong, but Melanchthon was not as ready to follow him without reservation as he had done before. Now he was going his own way. It is characteristic that he now turned again to Aristotle whom he had so strongly criticized at the peak of his literary activity in 1519-1520.[63] From this time on we can date the development of Melanchthon's independent theology.

The increased attention to his area of work in the philosophical faculty sharpened Melanchthon's view of the crisis which the university as an educational institution was then undergoing. Not only the Evangelically controlled universities, but also those with an unbroken Catholic attitude experienced a shocking drop in the number of new students. Comparing a representative cross section of the statistics for 1522 and 1527 makes this clear:[64]

|      | Cologne | Erfurt | Leipzig | Frankfurt on the Oder | Wittenberg |
|------|---------|--------|---------|-----------------------|------------|
| 1522 | 218     | 72     | 285     | 94                    | 285        |
| 1527 | 65      | 36     | 126     | 32                    | 73         |

Melanchthon did not only use his full energy reforming the structures of his own university, but also, with a host of textbooks and handbooks for the subjects he taught at Wittenberg, he attempted to reform the educational system of the Latin schools and even elementary schools. Not only the University of Wittenberg, but also those of Tübingen, Frankfurt on the Oder, Leipzig, Rostock, Heidelberg, Marburg, Königsberg, and Jena owe him either their new constitution or the new organization of their educational enterprise. A large number of grateful students assisted him, and their appreciation justly earned him the name of *Praeceptor Germaniae*.[65]

In addition there was the tireless activity of Melanchthon as the *ministerii evangelici membrum* (as he defined the task of the theological faculty); his hesitation to undertake theological teaching did not remove his ties to the church. He took an important part in everything that had significance in the Evangelical church. Until the Frankfurt Recess of 1558 or the Heidelberg Eucharistic Controversy of 1559 there was hardly a religious colloquy or meeting dealing with questions of the Evangelical church and theology, whether called by princes or theologians, in which Melanchthon did not take part, either personally or by preparing written opinions and reports. This was true not only of the "major" questions; one need only page through the collected letters in the Weimar Edition to find how numerous were the questions of ordinary church life in which Melanchthon, together with Luther and the other Wittenberg reformers, took an advisory or decisive part.

It is no coincidence that the *Instructions for the Visitors of Parish Pastors in Electoral Saxony* came from Melanchthon.[66] These *Instructions,* which deal with matters ranging from questions of doctrine to organizing the worship service and minute matters of school instruction, appeared for the first time in 1528. They grew out of the experiences of the first visitation—Melanchthon was the theologian member of the commission that carried it out—and provided a basis for systematic rebuilding of a new church structure. No less than ten editions of them appeared. In 1538-1539 their validity was extended to Ducal Saxony (five different printings) and in 1545 to Naumburg.

There can be no doubt that Melanchthon served the church with all his strength. But how great was that strength? When it came to practical defense in the face of danger, it failed him. After the defeat of the Smalcald War, when the emperor's supremacy had forced the Evangelicals into unendurable concessions, Melanchthon wrote a letter on April 28, 1548, to Carlowitz, chancellor to Maurice of Saxony. More revealing than the often-quoted sentences about Luther, [67] is this statement: "Perhaps I am by nature a servile character." [68] Some have tried to excuse this letter by saying that Melanchthon wrote it "while in a deep depression." But once again it revealed—and one must say it plainly—that Melanchthon was not capable of dealing with the stress of extreme situations. The German Lutherans attacked his surrender to Catholic demands with everything at their command and accused him—as they had in 1530—of betraying the gospel.

We do not want to document Melanchthon's weakness with words from German Lutherans only (who might be prejudiced), but also with the statement of an outsider. Calvin, although he was closely associated with Melanchthon and very dependent on his support, wrote a long letter to him on May 20, 1550. [69] More like "groaning than speaking" is this letter, which, although written by a friend, cannot exonerate Melanchthon of all his guilt and in which he can see "how severe the judgments of others are concerning you, and how offensive and unpleasant their remarks." [70] Some of the things that Melanchthon considers unimportant for the faith and thinks he can concede to the Catholics "are obviously repugnant to the Word of God.... You ought not to have made such large concessions to the Papists; because you have loosed what the Lord has bound in his Word, and partly because you have afforded occasion for bringing insult upon the gospel." [71] "And, indeed, good and pious men everywhere deplore that you should have countenanced those corruptions," so that the purity of the doctrine is contaminated and the church has faltered. In fact Calvin even supports Melanchthon's opponents, even though they are also his own: "I am not surprised that they became impatient when you abandoned them." While the emperor and the Catholics come after the Evangelicals "with savage rage . . . Philip sits in the enemy camp and keeps silent." [72]

In the deep crisis of the Evangelical church following the unfortunate outcome of the Smalcald War, not only the theologians, but also the congregations felt abandoned by Melanchthon. Emperor Charles V failed in his attempt to establish the Interim, the "temporary solution" for the German Evangelical church (until it was completely brought back to Catholicism). The resistance of the congregations, like that of the theologians, was too great and finally the revolt of the estates led by Maurice of Saxony put an end to Charles' political plans; it was in this context that the Peace of Augsburg could be attained in 1555 (cf. above, p. 53).

Melanchthon's position as the spokesman for German Protestantism and the prospect that he might be able to fill Luther's role after the latter's death in 1546 was demolished once and for all by his attitude in these controversies, especially since a number of other controversies were associated with them. These were all more internal theological concerns, revolving around the doctrine of justification (with Osiander and Mörlin), around the question of good works (chiefly between Melanchthon's students Major and Menius on one side and Flacius and Amsdorf on the other), around predestination and free will, i.e., about man's co-operation in salvation (chiefly between Melanchthon's student Pfeffinger and once again Flacius and Amsdorf), and finally about the interpretation and understanding of the Lord's Supper. These controversies were very unpleasant, not only because of the bitterness with which they were fought, but also because of the exaggeration of the viewpoints on both sides—and also because of the political contexts in which they took place. They finally led to the princes breaking free from the theologians and taking the initiative on their own to seek a way of uniting the hopelessly fragmented Lutheranism; the final result was the Formula of Concord and the Book of Concord of 1580, about which we spoke at the beginning (cf. above, pp. 57-58).

In connection with all of this occurred the decline of the Wittenberg theological faculty that had been dominated by Melanchthon. Here and in the entire university from 1546 on he was the undisputed head and the venerated master; for a long time the anniversary of his death was commemorated at the university with just as much ceremony as Luther's. But the lack of courage to speak his convictions clearly and to act on them, as well as the occasional need to deceive, led to ruin. As early as 1539 Calvin could say about Melanchthon: "As for himself, you need not doubt about him, but consider that he is entirely of the same opinion as ourselves." [73] He was referring to the understanding of the Lord's Supper.

In the 1540 edition of the Augsburg Confession, the so-called *Confessio Augustana Variata,* Melanchthon gave Article 10 on the Lord's Supper a markedly different wording (as he also did with Article 4 on justification). Here he wrote, *"With* the bread and wine the body and blood of Christ are truly tendered to those who eat in the Holy

Supper," where in 1530 had stood, "The body and blood of Christ are truly present and are distributed to those who eat in the Supper of the Lord," and a disapproval of all contrary teachings.[74] This was unmistakably opening the way to a weakening of Luther's position in the direction of Calvin's teaching (and it was not difficult to see why this Altered Augsburg Confession became the refuge of the Reformed church during the entire sixteenth century). Melanchthon had done the same thing with other doctrinal articles, but without publicly acknowledging his action or drawing the consequences; characteristic is Calvin's complaint in many of his letters: "How great are the weaknesses of this man, who will not say an open word even in the face of extreme necessity. For he agrees with us, but will not risk confessing his opinion publicly."[75]

The Wittenberg theological faculty proceeded similarly after Melanchthon's death. Thus it sank into ruin, for the Saxon elector desired to be a good and dutiful Lutheran. The faculty succeeded in making him believe that its attitude and teaching lay precisely along this line. The elector took this at face value and emphatically rejected the complaints against the Wittenberg faculty by the theological faculty at Jena, which had been newly organized after the Smalcald War as the protector of true Lutheranism. A great number of polemical pamphlets were exchanged, but when the elector became aware that the Wittenbergers were speaking with a forked tongue he acted with all the vanity and power of an absolute monarch who felt he had been deceived. In 1574 not only was the entire theological faculty newly staffed (except for Bugenhagen's professorship), but numerous other Wittenberg professors also lost their offices.

As could have been expected, with this intervention the decline of the university began, because the replacement professors were not chosen for their academic qualifications, but for their readiness to comply with the elector's wishes. Similar encroachments were repeated in 1581, 1588, and 1591, until the university was finally in line with rigid Lutheran orthodoxy.[76] As such it still enjoyed a great reputation at the beginning of the seventeenth century, since this viewpoint was in accord with the spirit of the times, but after that its star sank lower and lower. When it was finally closed in 1817 and united with the University of Halle which had constantly been rising since the end of the seventeenth century, this took place quietly without any echo in the German academic world, not to mention the international learned community.[77]

With the beginning of the destruction of Wittenberg's theological faculty in 1574, "Philipism" came to its end. The enduring influence of Melanchthon is correctly assessed by Richard Nürnberger:

> One should not assume that there will be a Melanchthon renaissance, like the Luther renaissance. Melanchthon has done his work. His influence has ended, no matter how intense it was in the late sixteenth and in the seventeenth centuries and how it molded the historical profile of German Lutheranism. What remains, i.e., what gives significance to studying the problem of Melanchthon, is the problem of his life work, the problematic of Protestant humanism.[78]

But that is not everything there is to say. Melanchthon is unusually difficult to evaluate because the discrepancy between his person and the claim of his office and work is so much greater than is the case with the other Reformers. All the Reformers have their failings and omissions. There are no saints in the Catholic sense here. Even if a person does all—and even more than—he is supposed to do, the words of Luke 17:10 still apply: "We are unworthy servants." The Reformers are not "substitute saints" for Protestants; they are men with all their weaknesses, just as theologians have always been. The only basis on which they should be judged is on what they have done and accomplished. In Melanchthon's case, we must look at the author of the Augsburg Confession and the Apology, not at the servile character who made so many bad mistakes.

On April 19, 1560, Philip Melanchthon died. Shortly before his death he summed up things on a scrap of paper. On one side he wrote, "You will be redeemed from sin, and set free from cares and from the fury of theologians," and on the other, "You will come to light, you will look upon God and his Son, you will understand the wonderful mysteries which you could not comprehend in this life: Why we were so made, and not otherwise, and in what the union of the two natures in Christ consists." [79] Although his strength was visibly waning, Melanchthon worked until the last moment. He was asked if he wanted anything. His answer, and his last word, was "Nothing but heaven, so ask me nothing more." [80] Thus Melanchthon died. The piety he here expressed and which ruled his entire life must also be considered when we judge Melanchthon.

# Ulrich Zwingli

~~~~~~~~~~~~~~~~~~~~~~~~~~~~~~~~~~~~

*Huldreich (Ulrich) Zwingli was born on January 1, 1484, in Wildhaus, county of Toggenburg, the third son of Ulrich Zwingli. After private instruction from his uncle, the dean Bartholomew Zwingli, he attended the Latin schools in Basel (1494-1496) and Bern (1496-1498). Family opposition made him leave the Dominican monastery in Bern (1498?), which he had entered as a novice. After his studies in Vienna (after 1498) and Basel (after 1502) had resulted in the Master of Arts degree, he turned to theology at the beginning of 1506, and by the end of 1506 Zwingli became people's priest in Glarus, a position he held until November 1, 1516. Then he took a leave of absence to assume the pastorate of Einsiedeln, a pilgrimage center, from which he went (after rejecting a call to Winterthur in 1517) to become people's priest at the Great Minster in Zurich in December, 1518. Here (as in Glarus) he pursued the study of ancient languages. After suffering from the plague from September to December, 1519, he composed his* Pestlied. *1520 was obviously the decisive year for Zwingli: The first reforms in Zurich, preparation of an interpretation of the Psalms, and, under Augustine's influence, a breakthrough from his previous humanistic attitude to a Reformation understanding of the Scriptures.*

*At the end of 1520 he gave up his rights to the papal pension (paid because of Zwingli's participation with Swiss mercenaries in the papal campaigns) and his external break in 1521 was marked by a public attack on his previous friend and patron Cardinal Schiner who was promoting such mercenary service. In his sermons (which from the very beginning were not expositions of pericopes, but of entire books of the Bible) Zwingli made preparations for the Reformation in Zurich, then introduced it in stages after 1522. Characteristic of this approach were the disputations accompanying each step. In the spring of 1522 Zwingli secretly married Anna Reinhart (made public by attending church together on April 2, 1524). In 1525 the Reformation was publicly introduced in Zurich by abolishing the mass (April 12), celebrating the Lord's Supper in both kinds (Easter), and enacting a marriage ordinance (May 10), followed by serious clashes with the dissatisfied radicals (Anabaptists).*

*The disputation in Baden (Oecolampadius against Eck and Faber) of 1526, in which the Catholic party triumphed, brought a setback, but the introduction of the Reformation in Bern after a disputation there in January, 1528 (and 1529 in Basel), more than compensated for it, although it increased the tension with the Catholic cantons. Attempts of each side to triumph through military action were hindered by the Peace of Kappel on June 26, 1529. Both sides tried to gain foreign allies; the Marburg Colloquy of October 1-4,*

*1529, was part of these attempts. On October 9, 1531,*
*the five Catholic territories declared war once again,*
*after Zurich had placed an embargo on shipments of*
*foodstuffs to them. At Kappel on October 11, 1531,*
*Zwingli fell in battle; his body was quartered and*
*burned by the hangman. Heinrich Bullinger took*
*over as his successor on December 9, 1531.*

~~~~~~~~~~~~~~~~~~~~~~~~~~~~

Luther and Calvin each had about 30 years for achieving
and shaping their Reformation activity; Zwingli, only 12.
The battle at Kappel in 1531 brought his work to an end.
His heritage did remain alive and the sphere of the Reformation's activity in Switzerland, for instance, expanded by
Geneva's becoming (with Bern's help) Evangelical territory.
But the Swiss Reformation attained new force through
Calvin's activity which eventually absorbed Zwingli's
church. In this way Geneva drew near to Zurich—as one
can see by studying its doctrine of the Lord's Supper, the
decisive point of contention among the Evangelical churches
during the sixteenth century—although the Reformed
church of the following years was defined by Calvin, not
Zwingli.

When one surveys the modern scholarly literature on
Zwingli, it is mainly by Swiss authors. One could thus get
the impression that Zwingli has only a local significance
for Switzerland, even more narrowly for German-speaking
Switzerland. This is far from true. It is of course an extreme exaggeration to say, "Anything more than Luther
that one finds in Calvin, comes from Zwingli," for, among
other things, Calvin did initiate and reorganize things for
himself. But one must not overlook the fact that the Swiss

Reformation already had a 16-year history before Calvin came to Geneva, and that this history was determined by Zwingli. Not only did Zwingli dominate the first epoch of the Reformation in Switzerland, but he also wielded made significant influence on the reformers in southern and southwestern Germany, of whom Martin Bucer is the most important. The influence of Zwingli and his students may be seen in Dutch theology and in the organization of the English state church. His activity extended to the German and international politics of his time, and it was his goal to create an anti-Habsburg, i.e., an anti-Catholic, European alliance. By no means was this plan as utopian as it sounds; if the German Lutherans had been more politically minded and had there been more men among them like Philip of Hesse, this alliance could have been realized.

The stage on which these plans came to nought was the religious colloquy at Marburg in 1529. In spite of all the efforts toward an agreement between the Swiss and German reformers, Luther and Zwingli could not reach agreement on the Lord's Supper, and the confessional differences hindered all further attempts. "You are of a different spirit," said Luther at this meeting, a word which lights up the situation like a lightning bolt. It applies to many, perhaps almost all areas, although one should not exaggerate the theological differences. The theologians at Marburg could nevertheless agree on 14 articles of doctrine (even though sometimes as a compromise), and only with the fifteenth article on the Lord's Supper did the disagreement become evident (Luther: "A sacrament of the true body and blood of Jesus Christ," in, with, and under bread and wine really eaten and drunk for the forgiveness of sin; Zwingli: "A sign of the true body and blood," given as a memorial to the congregation already certain of the forgiveness of sin through faith, celebrated as an obligation in thanksgiving for the redemption through Christ).

The Wittenberg Reformation began in 1517 with Luther's *Ninety-five Theses* and the dispute about indulgences. The Zurich Reformation began during the Lenten season of 1522 with Zurich citizens eating sausages in Zwingli's presence, i.e., with a provocative violation of Catholic ecclesiastical regulations. Zwingli's first real reformatory writing defended and explained this action: *On the Choice and Freedom of Foods*.[1] On July 2, 1522, Zwingli and ten other priests addressed a "Supplication" to the bishop of Constance, petitioning him for freedom to preach the Evangelical gospel and for priests to marry—several months earlier Zwingli had married secretly.[2] Three weeks later the Zurich council decided to permit Evangelical preaching. In November of the same year Zwingli resigned his office as people's priest at the Zurich Great Minster. On January 29, 1523, the first public disputation took place before 600 spectators. In *Sixty-seven Conclusions* (or theses) Zwingli presented his reformatory program, with its theological presuppositions and the practical consequences growing out of it.[3]

These *Sixty-seven Conclusions* have frequently been compared to Luther's *Ninety-five Theses*. There are external similarities in that Luther issued an explanation and enlargement of his theses in his *Explanations*,[4] while Zwingli also followed his *Sixty-seven Conclusions* a few months later with an extensive *Exposition and Proof of the Conclusions or Articles*.[5] With the contents, however, the parallels come to an end. Although Luther's *Ninety-five Theses* indirectly contained the entire foundation of the Reformation, they were written without that in mind, indeed without an inkling of it. On the other hand, Zwingli based his *Conclusions* on what had already taken place in Zurich, or at least had been attempted there, as the *Conclusions'* introduction [6] and the city council's invitation [7] to the disputation clearly show. It is because of this that the *Conclusions* have such an importance; they belong together with the *Exposition* (especially interesting are Article 18, with its demarcation from Luther, [8] and the appendix to Article 20 about his relation to Erasmus [9]) and the *Commentary on the True and False Religion* [10] of March, 1525, as Zwingli's most important reformatory writings.

Seven fundamental statements introduce Zwingli's *Conclusions:*

1. All who say that the gospel is invalid without the confirmation of the church err and slander God.

2. The sum and substance of the gospel is that our Lord Jesus Christ, the true Son of God, has made known to us the will of his heavenly Father, and has with his innocence released us from death and reconciled God.

3. Hence Christ is the only way to salvation for all who ever were, are, and shall be.

4. Who seeks or points out another door errs, yea, he is a murderer of souls and a thief.

5. Hence all who consider other teachings equal to or higher than the gospel err, and do not know what the gospel is.

6. For Jesus Christ is the guide and leader, promised by God to all human beings, which promise was fulfilled.

7. That he is an eternal salvation and head of all believers who are his body, but which is dead and can do nothing without him.[11]

On the basis of these fundamental theses, Zwingli then (Theses 8-10) draws this summary conclusion: Only the one who lives in Christ is a member of the church of God; whoever acts without Christ acts like a madman (11-12). If one listens to Christ he will learn God's will, so every Christian should use all his powers to see that only the gospel of Jesus Christ is preached, "for in the faith rests our salvation, and in unbelief our damnation" (13-14). When "in the gospel one learns that human doctrines and decrees do not aid in salvation" (16), [12] it will necessarily follow that all Catholic doctrines and institutions must be rejected: The Pope (17), the mass (18), intercession of the saints (19-21), good works (22), the temporal possessions and splendor of the clergy (23), [13] regulations about food (24), religious festivals and pilgrimages (25), monastic orders and celibacy (26-30), excommunication (31-32), and regulations about returning possessions illegitimately acquired (33). [14]

Position and repudiation are completely developed here, but Zwingli continues and discusses once more the most important points of distinction: Prayer (44-46), offenses (47-49), [15] forgiveness of sins (50-56), purgatory (57-60), [16] the priesthood (61-63), and the correction of abuses (64). [17] He inserted (34-43) [18] a series of theses concerning the magistrates, and this not by chance, for Zwingli was here addressing himself to the Zurich council which had a decisive role to play in the introduction of the Reformation. The so-called spiritual authority finds no basis in the teaching and actions of Christ for either its splendid way of life (34) or its usurped jurisdiction (36). This applies rather to the temporal authority (35), to which all Christians are to be obedient (37), as long as it does not demand something contrary to God's commandment (38). The laws enacted by such an authority should correspond in every respect to the divine will (39), and, if that is the case, the temporal magistrate has the right to impose the death penalty on those who give public offense (40). If, however, the temporal authority oversteps the limits set for the Christian, it may be deposed in accordance with God's will (42).

Zwingli ends his series of theses with an unmistakable threat: Whoever does not recognize his error will be judged according to God's justice (65).[19] All ecclesiastical officials should humble themselves at once and raise up the cross of Christ—not the money chest—or they will perish, since the ax is being laid to the root of the tree (66). Concerning questions of taking interest and paying tithes, of unbaptized children, or of confirmation Zwingli is prepared to initiate conversations (67), but "let no one undertake here to argue with sophistry or human foolishness, but come to the Scriptures to accept them as the judge," prepared to seek the truth or to maintain the truth already found. "Thus may God rule," concluded this programmatic "manifesto" of the Zurich Reformation; this is the only way to describe the *Sixty-seven Conclusions.*

Zwingli successfully defended his proposals against the objections of the vicar general of the bishop of Constance; the city council ordained that all clergy, under penalty of severe punishment for violations, should follow Zwingli's example and preach and act in accordance with the Scriptures.[20] In the fall of 1523 the convent of the Great Minster underwent reformation (in practical terms that meant conversion into an institution for the training of future clergy) and then on October 26-28 a second disputation dealt with the question of abolishing images and the mass.[21] In Janu-

ary, 1524, there was one more discussion—as always, under
the supervision of the city council—with the clergy of the
city about the introduction of the new measures which had
already been initiated step by step. The official decisions of
the council (May 14, 1524: Abolishing processions; April
12, 1525: Abolishing the mass) merely legitimized what was
already the general practice. In the fall of 1524 the Zurich
monasteries had been dissolved, and in May, 1525, a marriage ordinance was issued. Within three years the Reformation in Zurich had been accomplished in very direct and
consequential fashion, especially when compared to the
German Reformation which did not begin the systematic
organization of a new church until the visitations of 1526
and even then left many questions unresolved (e.g., marriage regulations) and in many others (e.g., worship services, images in the church) had stopped far short of Zurich.

There are two factors that are responsible for this "different spirit," this other way of acting. The first is that
Zwingli had never been the sort of strong Catholic that
Luther had, so that it was much easier for him to break
free from Catholicism. He had become a Catholic priest in
the "conventional" way, completely in line with his family
tradition. After completing the basic studies, becoming a
Master of Arts, and while still in the introductory stages
of theological study, he assumed his first pastorate in Glarus
in 1506 by purchasing it from the incumbent. Luther became a monk against his parents' wishes, after severe
internal struggles, in order to use every possible means
and power to propitiate God.

Zwingli conscientiously conducted his pastorate, but it did
not hinder him from intimate association with women.[22]
In Einsiedeln, where he assumed a position in 1516 and

engaged a substitute for Glarus, he again fell prey to this weakness after resisting for a year and a half. He confessed to this situation in connection with the negotiations for his call to Zurich where the matter had become known. He would indeed admit, he replied in his letter justifying the act, that the girl had borne his child, but he had not violated a virgin (a punishable offense), rather that the girl in question was the promiscuous daughter of a barber. "With deep shame," [23] he makes this confession; and he doubts "that he would in the future remain in the grasp of this evil habit." [24] But at the same time he adds, "I can promise nothing at all in this respect, however, mindful that I am encompassed by this weakness." This letter has only been known for a century and is not cited here to vilify Zwingli, but to illuminate his status at that time. This weakness did not damage his chances with the morally upright chapter in Zurich—countless other Catholic clergy were in much worse situations.[25] Zwingli received the position of people's priest without further ado.

The second factor which was then (and also later) determinative for Zwingli was humanism, which explains the relatively cool attitude of the letter just quoted (where he writes about the subject of guilt: "I have long ago asked forgiveness from the highest and best God;" and it is also said in the New Testament that even the righteous man falls seven times a day).[26] Of all the reformers (including Melanchthon) Zwingli was most strongly influenced by humanism. Luther had had only a fleeting contact with it and had never been influenced by its spirit. The humanistic influence had grasped Zwingli while he was still attending school and the university, and as a pastor in Glarus he was already a prominent member of the Swiss circle of humanists. Erasmus, whom Zwingli met in 1515, strengthened this attitude. He did break with Erasmus in 1523 over the latter's shabby treatment of Hutten—Zwingli offered the persecuted man the help and refuge which Erasmus had refused—but this did not mean a break with humanism as such.

When Zwingli was asked in 1526 about works that might offer help for a preacher, he listed a great number of ancient authors with special reference to the way in which they were useful, but he included no church father, no theological writing.[27] And when Zwingli depicted paradise for King Francis I of France, it contained not only the Old Testament heroes and New Testament apostles, but also "Hercules, Theseus, Socrates, Aristides, Antigonus, Numa, Camillus, Cato, Scipio." [28] It is only on the basis of humanistic presuppositions that some of Zwingli's theological opinions can be explained, his view in the hotly contested dispute about the Lord's Supper, for example.

Finally, Zwingli cannot be understood without the presuppositions of Swiss national politics. These matters were commonplace to him from childhood because of his father's position; as early as 1510 he began to take an active part in politics. At first he was concerned about the so-called "chasing after rice" and the pension practices connected with it, i.e., the mercenary service of Swiss soldiers for foreign powers and the open or secret payments these powers made to public officials or private individuals in Switzerland to secure support for their recruiting. Especially the pope and France were in constant competition for Swiss foot soldiers, considered at that time the most capable. Zwingli first attached himself to the papal side: Three times (1512, 1513, 1515) he went as a chaplain to Italy with a contingent of Swiss troops. His reward was to be named a papal acolyte chaplain and receive a papal "pension." When he left Glarus for Einsiedeln in 1516 it was because the pro-French party had gained the upper hand, and when he was called to Zurich in 1519 his political attitude also played a role. In the meantime Zwingli had developed under Erasmus' pacifistic influence into an opponent of "chasing after rice," and for the rest of his life he fought against it—with satisfactory results in Zurich, but in other cantons gaining bitter enemies for his efforts. These pensions were a comfortable source of income for the government, as well as for the upper classes. For many cantons the foreign mercenary service of their sons was also an economic necessity, because the poor soil could not produce enough to feed the populace. Thus the political differences were added to the religious differences over against the cantons which preserved the old faith. Then Bern adopted the Reformation and the balance of power tipped.

We have already spoken of Zwingli's political moves toward an alliance (cf. above, p. 84). His goal was to achieve an alliance against external powers as well as to create internal solidarity against the five Catholic cantons— Schwyz, Uri, Unterwalden, Lucerne, and Zug. It was intended to secure the expansion of the gospel and also the dominance of Zurich and Bern. The first War of Kappel, for which Zwingli—the former pacifist—had already been drawing plans since 1526, appeared to bring the decision in 1529. It was to Zwingli's extreme disappointment that it ended with an armistice. Tirelessly he agitated and prepared for a new war. When he finally accomplished his aim, Zurich was reluctant to go to war and poorly armed.

Strategic and tactical mistakes followed, and the battle at Kappel on October 11, 1531, brought total defeat.

Zwingli, accompanying the troops as a chaplain, took part in the battle and met his death as a soldier. The victors quartered and burned his body. On October 24, 1531, the opponents met once again at Gubel; although the Evangelicals now actually had superior strength, they were again defeated. Zwingli the politician had finally failed.

But Zwingli has gone down in history not as a Swiss politician, but as a Reformer. We have already spoken about the events of the Reformation in Zurich (cf. above, pp. 85-89), but what were the internal considerations which caused Zwingli to become a Reformer? When he was installed in his office of people's priest at the Zurich Minster on December 2, 1518, he was not yet a reformer in the strict sense of the word. With considerable stir he began his preaching activity with a continuing exposition of Matthew's Gospel (and when he concluded it, he began with other books of the Bible, thus violating the requirement to preach on the pericopes), but in his sermons we hear the student of Erasmus who wants to lead Christians to an Evangelical life by using Jesus as an example. Soon he fought against the indulgence preacher in Zurich, Bernhardin Sanson, but here again he bases his attack on the same source and does it completely in accord with the responsible ecclesiastical and temporal authorities. On the other hand, before November, 1519, Zwingli praised Luther as Elijah, the one who prepares the way of the kingdom of God, [29] and made sure that action was taken to disseminate Luther's writings widely, [30] and himself recommended them from the pulpit. At the end of 1518 we find Luther mentioned in Zwingli's correspondence for the first time, [31] and in such a way that we can presuppose even earlier information about him (perhaps an acquaintance with Luther's *Sermon on Indulgences and Grace* [32] of 1517).[33]

In the section on prayer in his extensive proofs of his *Sixty-seven Conclusions* of 1523 Zwingli appears to describe what brought him to the Reformation.[34] When he confronted the fifth petition, "Forgive us our trespasses, as we forgive those who trespass against us," it was as if he stood before a mountain; again and again he had to give in and he could never attain inner peace. After great difficulty he was finally able to accomplish the task of forgiving those who sinned against him, and he rejoiced over that. But soon he discovered his shallowness. For the fulfillment of the second clause did nothing to accomplish the first: "So I found that God was not obligated to act toward me as I was toward my enemy. And after much accusing and justifying of my poor conscience, I finally was so overwhelmed and captivated that I had to surrender myself to God. Lord, I dare not ask you to forgive me the way I forgive others. Lord, I am an enslaved man. Forgive me, Lord, forgive me!" Nothing but bare anxiety remained; Zwingli himself felt naked in this prayer, worn out by his stammering. When he turned to interpret a Psalm, his conscience told him: "Look, you shadow boxer! Here you think you are a man and are as pleased with yourself as if you had grasped the sense of the Spirit. If you are so bold, explain this: 'Forgive us our trespasses, as we forgive those who trespass against us.'" Everyone confronted with this petition of the Lord's Prayer must "confess and yield to the pure grace of God," is the way Zwingli concludes his statement. Walter Köhler regards this as fitting precisely into the latter half of 1520 when Zwingli was beginning his work on interpreting the Psalter: "In these lectures on the Psalms, if he did indeed ever deliver them, Zwingli represented Augustine's theology, a theology of justification by faith alone, a self-conscious Reformation faith." [35]

At that time, the second half of the year 1520, Zwingli had crossed the barrier that separated humanistic reform from the Reformation, and with Augustine's help the understanding of the entire Scriptures was opened to him, similar to the way Luther began (for his way had also led him through Augustine). Preparation for this lay in a severe onslaught of the plague in 1519, which had led to a deepening of his character both as a man and as a theologian.[36] He emphasized that he began to preach the gospel as early as 1516, even before he heard Luther's name, [37] and several times stressed his independence from Luther.[38] The majority of these statements come from the time following the Edict of Worms which threatened not only Luther, but all his adherents as well with the imperial ban and overban. Understandably enough Zwingli would make every effort to dissociate himself from Luther. In fact, however, Luther had provided Zwingli the decisive impulse for action and strongly influenced his theological development. Luther's example drove Zwingli forward, but he took the decisive step by himself—unless one can demonstrate a connection between Luther's lectures on the Psalms which began to be published in March, 1519, and Zwingli's beginning to interpret the Psalms in the latter half of 1520.

Zwingli's rejection of the papal "pension" at the end of 1520 (a painful decision for him, since he had previously financed his book purchases with it) [39] provides us with the final date of his break with the papal church, and from that time only a year and a half remained to prepare for the

Reformation of the Zurich church. For this purpose Zwingli chiefly used his sermons, which from the beginning were known for their effective interpretation of Scripture, and in biting polemics he evidently attacked abuses as if they were actual or potential opponents.[40] Thus, when it came to the realization of the Reformation from 1522 on, he had not only the majority of the preachers and the council, but above all the citizens of Zurich supporting him; only this can explain the rapid course of the Zurich Reformation. The generally accepted solution at that time was already that only what was based on Scripture could be valid in the church. After the Reformation's introduction Zwingli had the government in the palm of his hand and proceeded firmly against his Zurich opponents, of whom he was never free during his lifetime, with methods that were related to Calvin's. Everyone feared "being brought to the pulpit," i.e., being rebuked in Zwingli's sermons, and one must remember that after 1529 attendance at worship was obligatory. Zwingli's sort of moral control corresponded to Calvin's and the marriage tribunal as a court of morals (after 1526) prepared the way for the Genevan situation; in this way Zurich's Reformation flowed directly into Geneva's.

# John Calvin

*Jean Cauvin (Latinized as Johannes Calvinus) was born on July 10, 1509, in Noyon as the second child of the marriage of his father Gérard with Jeanne Lefranc. The father, first a notary of the local cathedral chapter and finally fiscal administrator of the Noyon diocese, originally intended that his son should study theology. Calvin received his first benefice at the age of 12 in 1521; a second, in 1527. In 1523 he began his studies in Paris, first at the Collège de la Marche, then at the Collège de Montaigue, becoming Licentiate of Arts at the beginning of 1528. From 1528 on, at the wish of his father, Calvin studied law in Orleans and Bourges (Licentiate in 1532, Doctor of Laws in 1533). After his father's death he turned to humanistic studies in Paris (entered Collège Fortel in 1532), and in 1532 produced his first writing, a commentary on Seneca's* De clementia.

*The time of Calvin's conversion to the Reformation, as well as the course of events leading up to it, is much disputed. The newly-elected rector of the University of*

Paris, Nicolas Cop, delivered his inaugural address on November 1, 1533. This address was composed by his friend John Calvin, and its evangelical character was so pronounced that both speaker and author were threatened with arrest. Both fled Paris and in 1534 Calvin gave up his benefices and wrote his first theological work, Psychopannychia (first printed in 1542, directed against the teaching of the dead sleeping until the resurrection). At the end of that year Calvin left France and went to Basel. Here the first edition of the Institutes of the Christian Religion took shape, and was published in 1536 with a preface to Francis I as an apology for the persecuted Evangelicals in France.

In 1536 (under the pseudonym of Charles d'Espeville) he went to stay in Ferrara, Italy, under the rule of Duchess Renée, followed by a brief, final stay in France. On the way to Strasbourg he made a detour (because of the war) through Geneva, where Guillaume Farel convinced him to remain, working first as Lecturer on the Holy Scriptures, then after a few months as Preacher. The attempt to give a new organization to the Genevan congregation was only partially successful. Eventually a conflict ensued with the council. On April 23, 1538, Calvin and Farel were ordered to leave the city within three days. Calvin went to Basel, but then in September was induced by Bucer to come to minister to the French refugee congregation in Strasbourg. Here appeared the second edition of the Institutes in 1539 and a commentary on Romans (the first of a long series) in 1540. Participation in the religious colloquies in Frankfurt (1539), Hagenau, Worms (1540), and Regensburg (1541) led to closer acquaintance with the situation of the church in Germany and to friendship with Melanchthon.

*In 1540 he married Idelette de Bure, the widow of an Anabaptist he had converted, and on September 13, 1541, he returned to Geneva. Now the congregation was reorganized according to Calvin's ideas, but serious battles with the old Genevans and the council erupted. Doctrinal disputes, in which Calvin engaged with might and main, accompanied these struggles. On June 5, 1559, the Genevan Academy, whose students worked as missionaries throughout Europe, was founded and in the same year the final edition of the* Institutes *appeared. In the following years he completed the series of biblical commentaries (only the Song of Solomon and Revelation were not treated), and on May 27, 1564, Calvin died after long years of suffering from many illnesses, to the end carrying out his manifold tasks with indefatigable energy.*

~~~~~~~~~~~~~~~~~~~~~~~~~~~~~~~~~~~~~~~~~~~~

"Every person, therefore, now sees that the strongest obligations of duty—obligations which I cannot evade—constrain me to meet your accusations, if I would not with manifest perfidy desert and betray a cause with which the Lord has entrusted me." With this statement Calvin gives reason for replying to Cardinal Sadolet, even though he held no official position at the time he wrote. The *Reply to Sadolet* was written in 1539 in Strasbourg after Calvin had been released by the Genevans, in fact—one might say—driven out in disgrace and shame. That was of no consequence to Calvin. He was only "for the present relieved of the charge of the Church of Geneva," he declared, for God "gave it to me in charge, having bound me to be faithful to it for ever." [1]

Calvin and his work can be understood only on the basis

of the *summa necessitas:* The tireless efforts he expended on behalf of his office, as well as the brazen consistency with which he withstood all opponents in Geneva during his 20-year endeavor to organize the church there on the basis of the will of God—an unshakable reality for him. In spite of all the complaints about the conditions in Geneva which one may find even in the later letters of Calvin, he succeeded in making Geneva a model of the new type of Reformation that spread throughout all Europe.

After the catastrophic defeat at Kappel in 1531 and Zwingli's death, the Zurich church was bereft of its power (the Consensus Tigurinus of 1549 was the first stage of its later amalgamation with Geneva). German Lutheranism, destroying itself in internal struggles, was principally concerned with preserving what already existed. It was in Geneva where the Reformed Church "according to God's Word" now came into actual existence with its radical, militant Christianity that did not shrink back from using the sword to defend its faith (the Hugenots in France, the "Beggars" in the Netherlands) or to establish it (the Puritans in England, the Presbyterians in Scotland). Although its moral strictness opposes the world, Reformed Christianity is surprisingly open to the world, even successful in the world. During Calvin's lifetime it spread through Switzerland, France, England, the Netherlands, a number of German territories, Hungary, and Poland, and today we find "Calvin's sons" in 75 nations, belonging to 127 churches with about 60 million members.

In contrast to Luther and Zwingli, Calvin might be said to have been born into the church. His father was an episcopal official. Calvin seemed destined to study theology and, at the age of 12, received his first ecclesiastical benefice.

It was not that his family lived without apparent tension with the church. Calvin's father died in 1531 while under the lesser excommunication, and in 1534 an ecclesiastical proceeding was initiated against his brother Charles. This has led some people to believe that the family's criticism of the church prepared Calvin for his way toward the Reformation. Such a simple explanation is certainly not true, for there is an unmistakable statement in Calvin's preface to his commentary on the Psalms of 1557 [2]—the single extended autobiographical report we possess—and it therefore carries even more weight since Calvin otherwise maintains silence about his development. [3]

Here Calvin reports very briefly about his youth. When he was a small boy his father determined that he should devote himself to theology, but later he changed his mind when he saw that the legal profession would make his son wealthier. In obedience to his father he then devoted himself to jurisprudence, until God in his secret providence directed him elsewhere. [4] Then comes the decisive passage:

> And first, since I was too obstinately devoted to the superstitions of Popery to be easily extricated from so profound an abyss of mire, God by a sudden conversion subdued and brought my mind to a teachable frame [*subita conversione ad docilitatem subegit*], which was more hardened in such matters than might have been expected from one at my early period of life. Having thus received some taste and knowledge of [not "about," as it is often translated] true godliness, I was immediately inflamed with so intense a desire to make progress therein, that although I did not altogether leave off other studies, I yet pursued them with less ardour.
>
> I was quite surprised to find that before a year had

elapsed, all who had any desire after purer doctrine were continually coming to me to learn, although I myself was as yet but a mere novice and tyro.... all my retreats were like public schools. In short, whilst my one great object was to live in seclusion without being known, God so led me about through different turnings and changes, that he never permitted me to rest in any place, until, in spite of my natural disposition, he brought me forth to public notice. Leaving my native country, France, I in fact retired into Germany, expressly for the purpose of being able to enjoy in some obscure corner the repose which I had always desired, and which had been so long denied me.[5]

If we summarize this report briefly we obtain the following result: This *subita conversio* led Calvin to something new; he was compelled to *docilitas* (this is not "the preliminary stage of faith," but rather the willingness to explore more deeply). This Calvin did with glowing zeal, and in less than a year (after the *subita conversio*) wherever he found himself (apparently he moved several times) he became a teacher of others who were inclined toward the Reformation and became a point for the crystalization of Evangelical congregations. This period of unrest ended when Calvin was "drawn into the bright light," i.e., became known publicly as a Protestant. The *subita conversio* and the following events are closely related; one cannot place the former in 1528 (and call it "a sudden conversion to the study of the Holy Scriptures") and date the "breakthrough to a Reformation consciousness" in the year 1533. Nothing but the second date is possible for this event, for only when it is accepted can Calvin's account be reconciled with the known dates of his biography: At the end of 1534 he went to Germany, i.e., Strasbourg, from which he traveled on to Basel; the previous months he spent at various places in France; a reformatory activity was already developing there (Angoulême, Nérac, Poitiers).

Naturally this *subita conversio* did not occur out of a clear blue sky; whoever wants to trace the course of Calvin's development to this goal must study his thinly disguised autobiographical presentation in the *Reply to Sadolet,* for it is not happenstance that Calvin there writes in the first person. Here he first describes—in words that remind one of Luther's account of his struggles in the monastery—his struggle with sin, his fear of the judging God, the ineffectual remedy of invoking the saints, the horror that could not be calmed by an act of restitution.[6] As an alternate way, nothing but "repression" was open to him, deceiving himself by trying everything in order to forget.

In the meantime, a new kind of teaching had been spreading (i.e., Luther's doctrine), which was quite different from the previous one.[7] Shocked by its novelty, Calvin only grudgingly gave it his ear, not merely because he did not want to admit that his entire life to this point had been in error and uncertainty, but primarily because of loyalty to the (Catholic) church. But soon he came to see things differently, for the representatives of this new faith convinced him that they were actually concerned about the good of the church. If Christ's rule were to be restored in the church, everything not based on what he had commanded in the Word of God must be abolished. In the papacy, the church's true form and the rule of Christ had been lost. Matthew 15:14, the passage about the blind man and his blind leader who both fell into the ditch, impressed

Calvin and removed his excuse that all of this was none of his business:

> My mind being now prepared for serious attention, I at length perceived, as if light had broken in upon me, in what a stye of error I had wallowed, and how much pollution and impurity I had thereby contracted. Being exceedingly alarmed at the misery into which I had fallen, and much more at that which threatened me in the view of eternal death, I, as in duty bound, made it my first business to betake myself to thy [God's] way, condemning my past life, not without groans and tears.[8]

This is the *subita conversio,* the first great turning-point in Calvin's life. It brought the *docilitas,* the receptiveness to God's voice, the beginning of the systematic formation of the new theology which found its initial major expression in the first edition of the *Institutes* in 1536. In its intention to serve as an apology for the persecuted French Protestants it was concerned with church practices, but it also belongs completely to the period of the inner education of the Reformer, who never in his life completed a conventional course of theological study. His complete devotion to practice began on August 5, 1536.

Calvin, while on a journey from Basel to Strasbourg, had stopped in Geneva—only for a night, he thought. Guillaume Farel, however, had heard about his stay in Geneva and hurried to the inn to get Calvin to make himself available to the Genevan church "not by persuasion or admonition, but by a frightful oath, so that I felt God had reached down from heaven and laid his hand on me with force." [9] Understandably Calvin did not feel himself equal to the task that Farel demanded of him, for he had never occupied an ecclesiastical office. He would rather have devoted himself to his private studies, but Farel broke his resistance: God would curse his studies, if Calvin did not help the church of Geneva in its need. Calvin stayed—until the end of his life; his three and a half year exile (April, 1538, to September, 1541) he regarded as a mere interruption, a "vacation" (cf. above, p. 99).

Calvin first began his work in Geneva without obligating himself to a particular office. But it was not long until he undertook to reorganize the Genevan church from the ground up. In 1537 the entire city was supposed to pledge itself to the true faith, which Calvin had summarized in the first Genevan Catechism.[10] The community, sworn to the true faith, was to stand under severe church discipline: Celebration of the Lord's Supper each Sunday, participation in it only by those who led a pure life, supervision of the congregation by people named by the council who would report all offences and vices to the pastor. He would then admonish the guilty parties fraternally and, if unsuccessful, report to the congregation with the ultimate consequence being exclusion from the Lord's Table—identical with exclusion from all association with the faithful—until such time as a real improvement took place. The council approved these articles, but removed the decisive part from them by limiting the celebration of the Lord's Supper to four Sundays during the year and by reserving for itself or its appointee the admonishment of the erring, especially the imposition of the penalty of excommunication.[11] The original decision was that whoever refused to take the oath of faith would have to leave Geneva, but the number of those who refused either to take the oath or to leave Geneva was so large that no one could compel them to do so.

Calvin thus failed in his first attempt; the further conflicts until the council ordered Calvin and Farel on April 23, 1538, to leave the city within three days was merely its consequence. When Calvin returned in 1541, because the Genevans knew no other way out but to recall him, the adoption of the *Ecclesiastical Ordinances* (which were revised several times until 1561) was a condition of that action.[12] The administration of the Genevan church was now divided into four offices: Pastors, teachers, elders, and deacons. The pastors were elected by their colleagues and the election was valid only when confirmed by the small council. Each week the Venerable Company of Pastors was to assemble for study of the Scriptures and the discussion following was supposed to clarify doctrinal differences; if they were unable to agree, the council should decide. That the pastors were subject to an especially strict disciplinary code is obvious. The office of teacher *(docteur),* which was ceremonially instituted, at first remained rudimentary. It was limited to general education until the Genevan Academy, incorporating and extending Calvin's previous teaching activity, was founded in 1559. The Genevan Academy very quickly became the central educational institution of the Reformed church, and in its international significance far surpassed even Wittenberg during Luther's lifetime. The deacons were responsible for the care of the poor. Most important, because it was characteristic of Geneva, was the office of the twelve elders *(anciens).* Selected from the council, they assembled with the pastors in a weekly consistory that supervised public order in the community. It had the assistance of the council which could impose penalties on those who resisted.

Thus private admonishment (which every member of

the congregation could exercise) was reinforced by the congregation's; whoever resisted would be punished by being excluded from the Lord's Supper. The list of punishable offences was wide-ranging. It extended from quarreling, slander, fraud in financial dealings, luxury in dress, theft, drunkenness, and "games, dances, and similar excesses which cause offence," to rebellion against the church order, false teaching, and blasphemy. From the beginning, a legal punishment was to be imposed for all of these offences in addition to the pastoral admonition.

Here church and state in fact merge, despite Calvin's attempts to keep them separate. The fact that the twelve lay members of the consistory were taken exclusively from the civil authorities (two from the small, four from the middle, and six from the great council) speaks for itself. In addition, very soon the chairmanship of the consistory devolved upon one of the mayors who conducted business in the presence of his mace, the symbol of temporal power. It was generally seen as one of Calvin's great achievements that an addition was made to the *Ecclesiastical Ordinances* in November, 1560, stating that the mayor had to leave his mace behind when he was in the consistory "to govern the church." [13]

The consistory also claimed the right of excommunication, but this was continually disputed, either directly or indirectly, by the council, the temporal authority, until the dispute about Philibert Berthelier clarified the situation. Berthelier, one of the leaders of the anti-Calvin party, had been excluded from the Lord's Supper by the consistory. On September 2, 1553, the council readmitted him to the Lord's Supper, despite Calvin's bitter opposition ("I would rather die than desecrate the holy meal of the Lord so shamefully").[14] Sunday, September 3, was the day of decision. But Berthelier did not approach the communion table; the council had secretly advised him not to. Calvin had triumphed (although he had to play his trump card—threatening to leave Geneva), but it was still several months before the council on January 24, 1555, expressly confirmed that the consistory had the right to excommunicate.

That was shortly before the final victory of Calvin (in the 1555 election the four mayoral offices were won by his supporters). The years preceding were filled with difficult struggles to maintain moral discipline. The greatest sensation was naturally caused by action against the upper class; it was handled with the same severity as the ordinary citizens, not an everyday occurrence in the sixteenth century. In the house of the city captain Perrin there was dancing in April, 1546; and "they were all cast into prison," the chairman of the consistory was removed, and a pastor who defended dancing lost his office and was imprisoned for three days. "He will afford a striking example," Calvin concluded in his report with satisfaction.[15]

A few weeks later Perrin laughed aloud (apparently somewhat irregular) at a wedding ceremony: "The mocker was held in close confinement [by the *council*] for eight days and then he had to confess his guilt before the congregation."[16] Ameaux, a member of the council, accused Calvin of being a wicked man who preached false doctrine. The council minutes from April 8, 1546, read: "Ameaux shall be sentenced to be led through the city streets, wearing a shirt and barefoot, and carrying a burning torch in his hand. Then he shall appear before the court, kneel, and beg God and his righteousness for forgiveness, and confess that he has spoken godlessly and maliciously."[17] On June

27, 1547, a placard threatening the preachers was found hanging on the pulpit of St. Peter's Church. Suspicion fell on Gruet; a search of his house disclosed incriminating papers, both politically and theologically.[18] Under torture he confessed the deed, was condemned to death, and beheaded.

"I do not defend my cause under the form of a public one, carried on in my absence," wrote Calvin to his friend Viret that month.[19] He explained to Ami Perrin that for no man's sake would he be swayed from the most conscientious observance of the law of his heavenly Lord.[20] Only on this basis can one understand Calvin's action in these disputes, as well as in the doctrinal proceedings at that time which generated even more public attention. We must deal with them in more detail, since they indicate the peculiarities of Calvin's theological position.

The controversy with Caroli on the Trinity and the creeds of the ancient church was only a preliminary event, and not merely because it took place in the first period of Calvin's Genevan activity. Caroli, who had fled from Paris to Lausanne, in January, 1537, had first accused Calvin of Arianism and then Sabellianism, because the words "Trinity" and "divine person" did not appear in the Geneva catechism. Calvin could refute this charge without difficulty; even though the words were not there, the teaching clearly was. Calvin successfully survived the doctrinal discussion in Lausanne; Caroli was removed from his pastorate. Nevertheless, as we can see in Calvin's letters, the matter aroused considerable attention and helped to weaken Calvin's position in Geneva. Caroli finally turned the discussion to the so-called Athanasian Creed; as long as Calvin refused to subscribe to it, he was suspect.[21] Even during

Calvin's stay at Strasbourg an extraordinarily bitter controversy broke out because of Caroli with the Strasbourg theologians, who naturally took offence at Calvin's refusal to subscribe to the ancient creeds of the church.[22] Nevertheless Calvin remained firm: The so-called Athanasian Creed did not come from Athanasius (on which he was undoubtedly correct) and also contained other errors which he could not accept.

The first controversy after Calvin's return to Geneva, the one with Castellio, was at first rather mild. Castellio, honored for his work with the Genevan schools, desired to enter the pastorate in 1544. The doctrinal examination in connection with his application showed complete agreement with Calvin, except for Calvin's interpretation of Christ's descent into hell in the Apostles' Creed (it was not to be taken literally, but to be understood as the pangs of hell which Christ had to suffer as he vicariously stood in our place before God's judgment seat), and the Song of Solomon which Castellio considered a secular love song which did not belong in the canon. In this Castellio—seen by today's standards—was correct, but Calvin emphatically opposed him, and Castellio was not permitted to enter the pastoral office (to one of his supporters Calvin declared that he would rather leave Geneva than allow Castellio to assume the office of proclaiming the Word "against the voice of [my] conscience").[23]

Castellio, however, was not expelled. He did not leave Geneva until July, 1544, after he had caused a bitter scene at a pastoral conference in May by expounding 2 Corinthians 6:4 in a way which, much to Calvin's anger, applied to the contemporary situation.[24] He found refuge in Basel—ultimately as a professor of Greek—and because of his experience became an opponent of Calvin from then on. After the trial of Servetus, he came out with a writing pleading for tolerance toward dissenters, which aroused a great deal of attention at that time and assured him a place among the defenders of the human spirit.[25]

This controversy dealt only peripherally with Calvin's doctrine and piety, but the next one went to its very center, the doctrine of predestination. Calvin emphatically taught double predestination (even if he, unlike Beza, put the *praedestinatio ad vitam* in the foreground), i.e., the doctrine that God elects people to good and to evil, to blessedness and to condemnation. This was similar to the way Augustine in the Pelagian controversy had developed the doctrine in its total bluntness, but which had subsequently never taken hold in the church. We are without influence over our election by God; God deals with us according to his inscrutable will. If we can be sure of our election we can also be sure of our salvation—from this certainty comes the particular strength and effectiveness of Reformed Christianity.

Jerome Bolsec, who after fleeing from Paris had lived near Geneva since 1551, attacked this position in the assembly of the Genevan pastors on October 16, 1551 ("the shameless man," "the good-for-nothing," "this pest," "this deceiver"), and "spit his poison out with an open mouth." [26] It is a godless opinion, he claimed, originated by Lorenzo Valla, that God is the cause of all things. Because we believe, we are chosen; only those who withdraw from the general offer of God's grace will be condemned.[27] A heated discussion followed, and at the close of the meeting a bailiff approached Bolsec and arrested him.

For the trial, opinions were requested from neighboring

churches. Basel, Zurich, and Bern, to Calvin's great disappointment and surprise, were quite reticent to express themselves. The doctrine of election was so difficult that one should compromise rather than take it to court right away. On December 23, 1551, Bolsec was expelled from Geneva. Later he returned to France and also to the Catholic faith. By means of the slanders and distortions in his biography of Calvin (first published in 1577),[28] he has influenced the picture of Calvin for centuries, much as Cochlaeus has done for Luther.

The case of Bolsec soon had a sequel. On September 1, 1552, Jean Trolliet, like Bolsec a former monk and now a translator for the Genevan council (after he had been prevented by Calvin's efforts from attaining the pastoral office), attacked Calvin's *Institutes* and his book on predestination which had appeared at the conclusion of the dispute with Bolsec and had achieved confessional character as the *Consensus Genevensis*. In his doctrine of predestination, according to Trolliet, Calvin was making God the author of sin. Calvin vigorously opposed him, but he was able to obtain nothing more from the council than a declaration of respect for himself and the *Institutes*. Among all his difficulties in Geneva, it is only this conflict about the doctrine of predestination, along with his struggles for church discipline, that Calvin recalls in the preface to his commentary on the Psalms, proof of how deeply it had affected him.

When one of his good old friends, Monsieur de Falais, expressed himself in favor of Bolsec (and apparently also of Castellio), Calvin sharply broke off their long-time relationship. He was sorry, wrote Calvin, that shortly before he had seen de Falais (while he still knew nothing of his attitude), and even if he came to Geneva a hundred times, "I will have less to do with you than with all my public enemies." [29] This Calvin would not write in an emotional rage, but while facing the danger of death from a serious illness. Calvin's commentary on 1 Corinthians had been dedicated to de Falais, but when the second edition appeared in 1556 he removed his name ("He will remain, as far as I am concerned, as one hidden in the grave," and it is right "that the man who has withdrawn from us will be forgotten," he wrote in the new dedication of the work to Marchese di Vico on January 24, 1556),[30] renewed evidence of Calvin's unrelenting severity.

The climax of this severity is generally considered to be Calvin's attitude in the trial of Servetus, who was burned at the stake in Geneva on October 27, 1553, for the crime of blasphemy. To the present day this episode casts a deep shadow in public opinion over Calvin's name. Noteworthy is the monument of expiation erected on the site of the execution in Geneva in 1903 at the 350th anniversary of the event, not by his opponents, but—as the inscription reads— by the "respectful and thankful sons of Calvin." It must be said that, according to contemporary law, Servetus would have suffered a heretic's death everywhere in Europe.

In 1531 the physician (discoverer, in the Western World, of the so-called lesser circulation of the blood) and passionate theologian published his book, *On the Errors of the Trinity,* and in 1533, *The Restitution of Christianity.*[31] Here not only was the doctrine of the Trinity denied, but in many ways the foundation of the Christian faith was attacked. According to the general conviction of the time such a heretic deserved death. Even Bolsec expressed his satisfaction at the death of "such a monstrous heretic, who was so evil and unworthy to live," and all the opinions Geneva solicited from the neighboring cantons spoke in favor of Servetus' execution. At the same time, as Calvin's defenders have rightly pointed out, throughout neighboring France the fires in which hundreds of Evangelicals died were flaming, not to mention the inquisition raging in the rest of Europe.

All of that is correct, but it is not the death of Servetus alone that must be laid to Calvin's charge, but the accompanying circumstances as well. The acquaintance of the two men went back 20 years; at first one had tried to convert the other (despite the danger, Calvin had traveled to Paris in 1534 to meet Servetus). When Servetus, who meanwhile resided in Vienne under the pseudonym of Villeneuve (in Spain the inquisition had initiated proceedings against him because of his first book), continued to storm him with letters, Calvin broke off the relationship: I have no doubt "that it was a devilish temptation of Satan to distract and withdraw me from other more useful reading." [32] At that time he was prepared, said Calvin, if Servetus came to Geneva (as he planned), "never [to] permit him to depart alive, provided my authority be of any avail." [33]

The correspondence of Calvin's friend Guillaume de Trie with his Catholic cousin in Lyons led to the catastrophe. At that time in Lyons five Swiss students had been thrown into prison as Protestants and were awaiting death at the stake. De Trie irritatedly wrote his cousin, who had reproached him for his conversion to the Reformation, that students were being burned in Lyons as false teachers while the prototype of all heretics lived undisturbed nearby and published blasphemous writings against Christianity. As proof he enclosed the first pages of *The Restitution of*

*Christianity*. In this poison pen letter—one can call it nothing else—Servetus' pseudonym was disclosed, but the grand inquisitor of Lyons, to whom the matter was immediately assigned, demanded (with consideration for the archbishop of Vienne, who possibly stood in close association with Servetus) incontrovertible proof, since both Servetus and the printer of the book denied it. Accordingly de Trie sent as proof the letters Servetus had written to Calvin, which he had importunately demanded from Calvin and the latter had given him with great reluctance.

Servetus was now arrested, but two days later was able to escape from prison. Nevertheless, he was condemned to death *in absentia* and symbolically burned in effigy, together with all the available copies of his writings. In his journey Servetus incomprehensibly went to Geneva, where he apparently found shelter among Calvin's opponents, and even more incomprehensibly attended a worship service conducted by Calvin. There he was recognized and, at Calvin's instigation, was arrested on the same day.[34] Calvin's secretary demanded the death penalty, and the formulation of the indictment obviously came from Calvin.[35] During the trial Servetus remained unbroken, and in his defense he demanded that "the false accuser" must "be exterminated as the sorcerer that he is, and driven out of your city. And his goods and property should become mine, since I have lost mine by his guilty act." [36] Nevertheless, the trial took its inevitable course; even Calvin's opponents in Geneva could not stop it. On August 20 Calvin wrote: "I hope for the death penalty at least; but I wish that the method of execution might be mitigated," i.e., decapitation instead of burning at the stake.[37] In November Calvin was already planning to write a work justifying his action, and the following year it appeared.[38]

This was the case of Servetus. It has been noted that the proceedings must be seen in the context of Calvin's struggle with his opponents. It has parallels to his argument over who had the right to excommunicate.[39] It is correct that the condemnation of Servetus came from the council, whose members were generally ill-disposed toward Calvin, and that it helped to weaken their position; in 1555 the pendulum finally swung to Calvin's side. But in arguing this way, one overlooks the fact that Calvin would not have dealt any differently, perhaps even more radically, with a council that was friendly toward him. He stated what motivated him in a letter to Simon Sulzer, the *antistes* in Basel: He considered it his duty, "to put a check, so far as I could, upon this most obstinate and ungovernable man, that his contagion might not spread farther." For godlessness and governmental indolence everywhere hindered the "vindication of the glory of his [God's] name." He certainly did not want to imitate the furies of the inquisition, "but there is some ground for restraining the impious from uttering whatever blasphemies they please with impunity." [40]

Even before the trial of Servetus, Calvin was involved in the last great controversy of his life—with the German Lutherans over the Lord's Supper. In the beginning Calvin had been without doubt a pupil of Luther, as the first edition of the *Institutes* in 1536, which was modeled after Luther's Small Catechism, gives clear evidence. Even his *Short Treatise on the Holy Supper of Our Lord* of 1541 shows how much he inclines toward Luther in the doctrine of the Lord's Supper, the decisive point of difference between Luther and Zwingli.[41] Unquestionably Luther was for him far superior to Zwingli, against whom he at first directed a strong critique.[42] Nevertheless we find him becoming more and more critical of Luther's strong attitude against the Zurich theologians.[43] After the conclusion of the *Consensus Tigurinus* of 1549—a decisive development for the Reformed church—Calvin assumed a final position in sharp opposition to "Luther's monkeys."[44]

Luther's view that all communicants, even unbelievers, receive the true body and blood of Christ (*manducatio oralis et impiorum*) is just as wrong, according to Calvin, as the presupposition which lies behind that view—the doctrine of Christ's ubiquity (the ability to be present everywhere). As the Scriptures and the ancient church testify, Christ is in heaven according to his human nature, and therefore cannot be present with his flesh and blood in the Supper. The notion of a real eating of his body and drinking of his blood cannot be held, especially if an unbeliever can do it. Calvin also acknowledges that believers really and substantially receive Christ's body and blood in the Lord's Supper, but it is only their power which is communicated to them through Christ's spirit. The crucified Christ is the content, the substance of the Lord's Supper; the power that the participants here receive is the reconciliation, the new life. Thus Calvin can indeed subscribe to the Augsburg Confession, not the *Invariata* of 1530, but the *Variata* of 1540 ("in the sense in which its author meant it," i.e., Melanchthon, who had altered his original statement in Article 10 about the real presence in the Lord's Supper).[45]

Against these views of Calvin, who knew how to ridicule the faith in "the God in the bread,"[46] came an extraordinarily severe attack from "the icy North Sea,"[47] i.e., from Joachim Westphal, a chief pastor in Hamburg.[48] The gulf between Lutherans and Reformed grew deeper once again, and it is only our own generation which has begun to build bridges over the places where that gulf still exists and has not already been filled in by historical developments.

Calvin's death on May 27, 1564, brought no essential change for the church in Geneva. It remained for a long time just the way it had been during his lifetime—proof that this was not the tyranny of one-man rule, even though the many arguments and conflicts might have made it appear so to a posterity influenced by a partisan writing of history. At that time the Reformed faith was on the march everywhere. In 1566 the Netherlands began its struggle for freedom from the Spanish yoke; in 1567 the civil war that cost Mary Stuart her throne broke out in Scotland; in 1570 the Huguenots won the peace of Saint-Germain-en-Laye and in 1598 the Edict of Nantes.

But the Reformed church also suffered severe losses from the attacks of the Counter Reformation, first in eastern Europe and then increasingly during the course of the seventeenth century in France, until the involvement of the Huguenots in the French political disputes and the influence of the Jesuits on Louis XIV brought their existence to a tragic end. Because of this the French component in Reformed Christianity was decidedly weakened, while the Dutch, the English, and increasingly also the German component gained strength within the Reformed church, which however, following Lutheranism's example, became characterized by a theology of orthodoxy that made up in doctrinal disputes for everything neglected earlier. Here the teaching of Calvin became Calvinism, just as Luther's

had earlier become Lutheranism, both with loud appeals
to the spiritual fathers but yet diverging from their inten-
tions, whether in limiting their teachings or in expanding
them to unrelated subjects. Nevertheless it appears—at least
to one who stands in the heritage of Luther—that this
limitation or expansion of the succeeding years has been
stronger in Lutheranism than in Calvinism.

A well-known Calvin scholar once confessed that in his
early years he warmed up to the theme of Calvin only
when he could express his indignation of the way Calvin
handled his opponents. That attitude changed funda-
mentally when he confronted Calvin more closely, a development which everyone who earnestly occupies himself
with Calvin will also experience. Unfortunately there is no
extensive biography that can command universal acceptance on the strength of its objectivity and knowledge of
the subject. The critics of Calvin—from Bolsec in the sixteenth century to Kampschulte at the close of the nine-
teenth—have had more success than his defenders; their
apologetic stands in the way of the desired effect. The
numerous recent biographies of Calvin all have this same
problem. Yet, the confrontation with Calvin will be difficult
for modern readers even if such a definitive biography, for
which we urgently hope, appears. Calvin, who believed that
zeal for God's glory was fundamental for the living of our
life—for we were born for God and not for ourselves—can
only be fully grasped and evaluated when we, at least in
principle, recognize this as valid for ourselves.[49]

# Postscript

This volume has presented the life and work of the four great Reformers; it has not given a history of the Reformation. Nevertheless, it may be helpful to provide a brief supplementary word in which some important points may be raised in order to prevent our making incorrect or incomplete judgments about the Reformation.

## 1. THE REFORMATION OUTSIDE GERMANY AND SWITZERLAND

It is clear enough on the basis of what we have already said that the Reformation had two centers (at least two—we shall speak later about the "third force," cf. below, pp. 129-133); the well-known phrase, "Germany, the homeland of the Reformation," is only partially true. It becomes quite clear that the Reformation is not a German—or a Swiss—event, but a European one, when one observes the Reformation beyond the borders of those two lands. Luther's Reformation won a foothold in eastern Europe, but in the long run endured only in the north, in Scandinavia. In the romance-language countries it had little success and was quickly replaced by Calvin's Reformation, as it was in England and Scotland which experienced their own Reformation history. The French-speaking lands were soon completely dominated by Calvin's Reformation. The reasons for this situation cannot be found in a special disposition of these peoples—"ethnic spirit" or even "race"—which sought a particular form of Reformation, as some have tried to do. The reasons are of a different sort.

It was partly the tyranny of the state that completely crushed the beginnings of the Reformation or kept it small. That was the case in Spain, where small Lutheran groups gathered in Valladolid and Seville until the inquisition eliminated or scattered them after 1559. In Italy the Reformation had the support of the court in Ferrara. It had centers in Venice and Naples, but from the beginning had a difficult time there with the populace which supported the papacy for nationalistic reasons (although it was possible for the papal legate to Germany, Vergerio, the bishop of Capo d'Istria, to defect to the Reformation). As in Spain and France, it was the humanistic intelligensia in Italy which felt itself close to the Reformation, without clearly deciding for it. They proved to be a considerable obstacle to the Reformation's spread, since it seemed possible to them through symbolic reinterpretation of Catholicism to evade what otherwise might have been a serious conflict (it was not in jest that Calvin raged against the "Nicodemites"). Thus the Reformation developed very slowly in Italy.

After Luther's death the influence proceeding from

Wittenberg was decisively reduced. Melanchthon, the Lutheran leader, was attacked, and the Lutherans feuded among themselves, even though German Lutheranism was fighting for its very existence. This is the time of Calvin's victory in Geneva which made the Genevan Academy the educational center of the Reformation. It was from Geneva, not Wittenberg, that growth of the Reformation outside Germany proceeded, and anyone educated in Geneva was inevitably stamped with the severity and energy of Calvin and his Reformation. This gave Reformed Christianity a headstart over Lutheranism. In France and present-day Belgium the language similarity gave Calvin's Reformation an obvious advantage. Calvin had directed all his efforts toward extending the Reformation in his homeland. The allegiance of the Waldensians in Italy to the Swiss Reformation is explained by their proximity to Geneva.

In the northern lands (whose political unity, existing since 1397, was beginning to crumble), the Reformation first put down roots in Denmark. As early as 1520 emissaries from Wittenberg were in the country, the New Testament appeared in the vernacular in 1524, and after 1526 Frederick I publicly promoted the Reformation. Twenty-one Lutheran clergy presented the *Confessio Hafnica* as their confession of faith in 1530, and in 1536 the parliament decreed the introduction of Lutheranism as the state religion. As the emissary of Wittenberg, Bugenhagen gave assistance in the internal and external organization of the church.

In Sweden Olaf Petersson (Olaus Petri), a student at Wittenberg, was the leader of the Reformation (the Danish reformer Hans Tausen had also studied at Wittenberg). The victory of the Reformation, which was promoted by Gustavus Vasa, elected king in 1523, is associated with the struggle for Swedish independence, and, as a result, the connection between church and state became very close. The basic decision was made by the parliament at Västerås in 1527. The final accomplishment of the Reformation took much longer, however. In 1528 a reorganization of dioceses was effected, in 1536 celibacy was abolished, in 1539 the German, Georg Normann, was called to lead the Swedish church, and in 1544 the parliament at Västerås pledged to hold fast to the Reformation for all time.

Finland, which was allied with Sweden, followed the same development. Here also Wittenberg students took a significant part (Michael Agricola). In Norway the Reformation was introduced by Denmark from above and did not grow from the grassroots; assemblies of notables adopted the Danish-Norwegian Church Ordinance in 1539.

Due to the person and actions of Henry VIII (1509-1547), the English Reformation followed its own changeful course, directed by the king's passions and moods. Yet nevertheless there were relations with Wittenberg (an English legation visited in 1535, and in 1524-1525 Tyndale there translated the New Testament into English, which was distributed together with Luther's writings), but at first not much more resulted than a break with Rome and the creation of a state church under the monarch (Supremacy Act of 1534). Under Edward VI (1547-1553) the Reformation took its first real steps. The Short Instruction was issued in 1548, the Book of Common Prayer in 1549, and it was revised in 1552 under the influence of Evangelical refugees from the continent (Bucer, Peter Martyr, and others). The confession of faith in the Forty-two Articles indicates a stronger and stronger Calvinistic influence in the Reformation's development.

The attempt to reestablish the Catholic church in England

under Mary (1553-1558) failed, and finally the Anglican church was consolidated under Elizabeth I (1558-1603), although Puritan congregations which wanted a more radical development of the Reformation already existed everywhere. In Scotland the Reformation began under Lutheran influences (Patrick Hamilton, a Wittenberg student in 1527, was burned at the stake at St. Andrews for his stand in favor of the Reformation), but then received its Presbyterian character through the work of John Knox (1505-1572), certainly the most illustrious graduate of the Genevan Academy. In 1560 parliament adopted the *Confessio Scoticana*.

In Hungary, as well as in Siebenbürgen and Poland, the Lutheran Reformation had its strongholds in the German cities and settlements, but even the native nobility sent their sons to Wittenberg. In Hungary the entire nobility, except for the families of three magnates, endorsed the Reformation, and in Siebenbürgen complete religious freedom was declared in 1534. However, from the 1550s on, Calvinism made steady inroads everywhere and Melanchthon's students also followed it. Thus it came to various schisms, especially in Poland where the groups adhering to the Reformation were almost hopelessly divided. All in all, however, the victory was generally won by Calvin's Reformation whenever it was not directly opposed by a revived Catholicism (e.g., in Poland).

In France, Calvin's Reformation found support principally from Margarete of Navarre and her daughter Jeanne d'Albert, but also from the higher nobility. Although the Star Chamber imposed the death penalty on hundreds of people after 1547, the Reformation continued to spread. Congregations began to be organized in Paris in 1555, and by 1559 there were 72 congregations, almost all of whose pastors had been educated in Geneva. The list which Admiral Gaspard de Coligny, the Huguenot leader, presented to Catherine de Medici in 1561 counted 2150 congregations. In 1559 the first national synod met and adopted the *Confessio Gallicana.*

In the Netherlands the Reformation was spread by refugees from France and also by emissaries from Geneva. It was at first put down by bloody persecution. Here the first martyrdoms of the Reformation took place: Henry Vos and John of Esch from the Augustinian monastery in Antwerp were burned at the stake in Brussels in 1523; Jacob Propst and Henry of Zütphen, both Wittenberg students, managed to flee. The *Confessio Belgica,* which was written by the Geneva-educated Guido de Bray in 1561, was adopted as a statement of faith by a synod in Antwerp in 1566. It became the bond of unity for these congregations that had to suffer severe persecution because of their location within the Spanish hereditary lands, until they finally achieved their independence at the same time as did their nation.

## 2. THE "LESSER" REFORMERS

It is understandable, in view of Luther's importance, that those alongside him are often neglected. But it is unjust, and it also obscures the historical development of the Reformation. The Reformation was spread by countless unknown preachers, won through reading Luther's writings or studying the Bible, who gave up their Catholic pastorates or left their orders and preached the gospel to new congregations. Often they afterward went to Wittenberg for further study, and soon the normal route into the Evangelical ministry was exclusively through the Wittenberg theological faculty (and, after 1527, also through the faculty at Marburg and other universities). Each one of them attracted others and soon centers of the Reformation grew up in various provinces of Germany. Here there were people at work who had an independent significance alongside Luther, even though they frequently were dependent on him. We must speak about them, although only selectively and all too briefly, lest the picture of Luther's Reformation appear incomplete.

Many of them had a close personal relationship to Luther. Johann Lang (c. 1487-1548, Erfurt's reformer and advisor of his prince in the Schwarzburg territory) and Wenceslas Linck (1483-1547, reformer of Altenburg, then later of Nuremberg, who took part in the religious colloquies in Hagenau and Worms) had been Luther's brethren in the monasteries at Erfurt and Wittenberg. George Spalatin (1484-1545), the court preacher of Frederick the Wise, played a key role in the Reformation's early stages. He was Luther's intermediary with the elector (with whom Luther never spoke personally) and represented the Reformation cause at court. He also served Frederick's successors as an advisor while he was superintendent in Altenburg and, beyond that, was frequently used in the visitations and diplomatic negotiations concerning religious affairs.

Among Luther's colleagues at the university, Justus Jonas (1493-1555) and Nicholas von Amsdorf (1483-1565) helped to introduce the Reformation into Wittenberg. Jonas, the reformer of Halle, was present at all the important diets and had an extensive part in the reorganization of the church in Electoral Saxony. He wrote various church orders and translated numerous writings of Luther and Melanchthon. Amsdorf was Luther's close confidant and was with him at the Leipzig Debate in 1519 and at the Diet of Worms in 1521. He directed the introduction of the Reformation in Magdeburg, Goslar, Einbeck, and other places, always representing its right wing; after Luther's death he became the spokesman of radical Lutheranism.

Johannes Bugenhagen (1485-1558) first came to Wittenberg in 1521 as a student. He stood close to Luther as a professor on the faculty and then as pastor of the City Church; Luther often substituted for him in the pulpit when Bugenhagen was away, as he frequently was, strengthening the Reformation in other places. Brunswick, Hamburg, Lübeck, Pommerania, Denmark, Holstein, and Hildesheim received their church ordinances from him. Nicholaus Hausmann (1478/79-1538, reformer of Zwickau and Dessau) had the closest relationship to Luther; the *German Mass,* the visitations, and Luther's catechisms were at least partially done at his initiative.

Among those who sat at Luther's table should be mentioned Conrad Cordatus (1475-1546, especially known for his transcription of Luther's Table Talk) and Veit Dietrich (1506-1549, preacher in Nuremberg, collector of Luther's Table Talk and sermons, editor of the Postils, author of important practical and theological works).

The names of Wittenberg students such as Johann Hess (1490-1547, reformer of Breslau and Silesia), Johannes Briesmann (1488-1550, reformer of Riga and Samland), and Johannes Mathesius (1504-1565, pastor in Joachimsthal in Bohemia and the first of Luther's biographers) may illustrate how extensive the influence of the Wittenberg faculty extended throughout the German-speaking world; Wittenberg students were also among the leaders of the Reformation in Hungary, Scotland, and Scandinavia.

As early as the Heidelberg Disputation of 1518 Luther had won followers and sympathizers in southern Germany, among them Erhard Schnepf (1495-1558, one of the reformers of Württemberg, a participant in the religious colloquies at Hagenau, Worms, and Regensburg), Johannes Brenz (1499-1570, responsible for Württemberg's "second Reformation," the church ordinance of 1559), and Martin Bucer (1491-1551). Brenz belongs to the representatives of Lutheranism in southern Germany, and Bucer to the type of Protestantism midway between Lutheranism and the upper German form more influenced by Zwingli. It was largely due to Bucer, whom Luther frequently mistrusted, that the Wittenberg Concord of 1536 came into existence. Bucer, the leader of the Strasbourg church along with Wolfgang Capito (1478-1541) and Caspar Hedio (1494-1552), took part in all important theological discussions and colloquies of the Reformation period. After the Interim he went into exile in England, where in Cambridge he quickly won influence in the university and also in the English church.

## 3. THE "LEFT WING" OF THE REFORMATION: ANABAPTISTS AND SPIRITUALISTS

From the beginning the Anabaptist and Spiritualist element was alive and active in the Reformation, both in Germany and Switzerland; any treatment of the Reformation that did not consider these elements would be incomplete. Yet nowhere in Reformation studies is the picture more complex; it is virtually impossible to view the many diverse and often contradictory elements as a whole. The movement's roots extend back beyond the Reformation into the late Middle Ages with its atmosphere of spiritualism, apocalypticism, and social revolution. Common to all of its branches was its radical commitment to its convictions, and its opinion that the Reformation had stalled halfway to its goal; it had grown tired too soon and had become a bourgeoise movement. Thus the "left wing" became the conscience of the Reformation. This movement which intended to gather the "communion of saints" must always be seen as a check, even though others will never be able to follow fully the demands it makes and the solutions it proposes.

Some definite general characteristics may, however, be mentioned. The most obvious was the rejection of infant baptism. Important also was the social revolutionary component which diminished after the catastrophe of the Peasants' War (in which many members of the movement had taken part) and the Anabaptist kingdom in Münster. It did not have to appear in that fashion; the example of Jacob Hutter and his *Brüderhof* in Moravia and the "Communistic" Christian community that grew from his work is proof of another type.

The mystical-spiritual line is also clear. Beside the Scriptures, mystical contemplation is a source of revelation, and this "inner light" clarifies and goes even deeper than the Scriptures. The apocalyptic character was not found everywhere, but it experienced a renewed strengthening in the face of persecutions. Melchior Hofmann may serve as a typical representative. In 1529, after many years of wandering and severe conflicts, Hofmann came to Strasbourg where he found the "key of David" to interpret the secret revelation of God in the Bible. As the apostle of the last days he announced the world would end in 1533. Expelled from

Strasbourg, he filled all of Germany with his passionate apocalyptic preaching. Believing himself one of the witnesses of the last days foretold in Revelation 11, he returned to Strasbourg where he was imprisoned until his death in 1543 without giving up his conviction.

Luther's Reformation faced this movement as early as 1521, when the Zwickau prophets attempted to influence events in Wittenberg during Luther's absence. In 1525 Luther came to a sharp confrontation with it in the person of Karlstadt; he also confronted it in Thomas Müntzer and the circles influenced by him. In contrast, he had no significant conflict with the Anabaptist movement. Luther first took a stand on the question of infant baptism in 1525 (in the Lenten Postil), and in 1528 he could still state (in *Concerning Rebaptism,* written to two pastors) that he did not know the Anabaptists' arguments from firsthand experience.

It was quite different with Zwingli. In 1523-1524, infant baptism had already been attacked or even omitted in Saint Gallen and in Zurich. When the Zurich council issued a mandate in January, 1525, that all omitted baptisms had to be performed within eight days, the result was that, among other things, mobs overturned the baptismal fonts. In March, 1526, the penalty of drowning was prescribed for so-called rebaptism and was imposed on Felix Manz in 1527. Blaurock and Grebel in Switzerland, Balthasar Hubmaier in Waldshut (later at Nikolsburg in Moravia with a congregation of 12,000 believers), Hans Denck in Nuremberg, and Ludwig Hätzer in Augsburg were the first to proclaim the demand for adult baptism, since infant baptism, the "antichristian water bath," was contrary to the Scriptures.

In addition to Switzerland and Nikolsburg in Moravia, the movement had its center until 1528 in Augsburg (here

the "martyr synod" took place in 1527 under Denck's leadership), then until 1533 in Strasbourg (here Bucer's religious
colloquy with Pilgram Marpeck took place in 1532), and
finally (due to Marpeck's activity) once again in Augsburg.
But congregations were also formed in central and northern
Germany (Münster) and along the lower Rhine, for the
itinerant preachers of this new doctrine were everywhere.
Authorities of all confessional persuasions—the usual conception that this was only an intra-protestant controversy
does not accord with the facts—acted with equal brutality,
after the law concerning heretics was proclaimed against
them, first by the emperor in 1528, and then by the estates
at the Diets of Speyer in 1529 and Augsburg in 1530.

The events at Münster appeared to justify that action.
There at the beginning was the activity of Bernd Roth-
mann. When Jan Mathys from Haarlem and Jan Beuckel-
son from Leiden joined him in 1534, the movement, reinforced by adherents from Holland, Frisia, and the lower
Rhine, was able to gain control of the city and began to
establish the "kingdom of God." This resulted in despotism
and bloodshed.

Yet Anabaptism dare not be seen only from this perspec-
tive. It is also aware of the demand of pacifism, as is demon-
strated by Menno Simons who, in 1536, began to invite
Anabaptists to Groningen after the catastrophe at Münster.
He then extended his activity to northern Germany, the
lower Rhine, and even to West Prussia. Simons gathered
a free-will Anabaptist congregation freed from shadows of
the past, purified from the remnants of Catholicism. Its
members intended to live in complete accord with the
Scriptures and demanded that a confession of faith bring
forth visible fruit. In other places a purging also occurred;

the German and Swiss Anabaptists returned to the decisions made at the Anabaptist council at Schleitheim in 1527, although in the succeeding years their communities grew smaller or returned entirely to the territorial churches.

Although they had learned much from Anabaptism, the pure spiritualists such as Sebastian Franck (1499-1542) and Kaspar von Schwenckfeld (1489-1561) had previously separated from it and had begun to form the spiritual church, a fourth type alongside the three confessions (which contained Anabaptists), an invisible community known to God alone, which alone would lead people into blessed fellowship with Christ. By 1550 three main groups of Anabaptists were in existence: The Swiss Brethren and the Hutterites in the south, with the latter also in Moravia, and the Mennonites in northern Germany and the Netherlands. The Anabaptist group in Poland was organized later and then merged into Socinianism, while the other groups exist to the present day (in areas as far away as Russia and North America).

## 4. REFORMATION "FROM THE TOP DOWN" OR "FROM THE BOTTOM UP"?

One of the most widespread judgments is that the Reformation was introduced "from the top down," especially in the Lutheran areas. One can adduce these facts, for example, as proof of such a thesis: The Reformation in Württemberg did not succeed until Duke Ulrich was restored to the throne and in Saxony it was not until after the death of Duke George that the Reformation triumphed under his brother Henry, and then not completely until his son Maurice came to power. Hesse under Landgrave Philip may serve as another example. The necessary condition for the introduction of the new faith into a territory seems to be the conversion of the ruler. But, in fact, something quite different is the case. In Ducal Saxony the Reformation was brutally repressed by Duke George. Under his successor Henry, it was tolerated, and then it blossomed. Maurice only tied together what had previously grown. The same thing happened in Brandenburg. Joachim I's role corresponds exactly to that of Duke George of Saxony; Joachim II's, that of Duke Henry. It was similar in Württemberg. When Duke Ulrich regained his position, the dam which until then had held back the spread of the new faith was breached.

A glimpse of the center of the Lutheran Reformation, Electoral Saxony, will make clear that this "from the top down" thesis of many historians is extremely questionable. On one hand they declare that Elector Frederick the Wise had no inner commitment to the Reformation, while on the other hand they think that the Reformation was introduced into his territory by the temporal government. This will not work, unless they resort to the claim that the princes only promoted the Reformation because they coveted the church property. But that will not fit either the person or the action of Frederick the Wise.

The only possible explanation for the events in Electoral Saxony—and in other places as well—is that the Reformation did not develop "from the top down," but exactly the other way around, "from the bottom up." Frederick the Wise did indeed perform decisive service for the Reformation in deciding not to surrender Luther to Rome or to the empire. But in connection with the introduction of the Reformation in his territory, in every instance he merely acceded to Luther's stormy pressure; his advisors who had been captivated early by the Reformation (including Prince John Frederick) pushed him into doing so. What happened with the All Saints foundation in Wittenberg is typical. Its members defended the old confession with every means at their disposal; they had to surrender to the attacks of Luther and the Wittenberg populace, even though the elector attempted to protect them because of his fear of the consequences from the imperial law.

The events in the cities are the final proof that the growth of the Reformation proceeded from the community. "There was no city council Reformation," has been clearly established for the north German cities (Franz Lau, "Der Bauernkrieg und das angebliche Ende der lutherischen Reformation als spontaner Volksbewegung," *Luther-Jahrbuch*, 26 [1959]:109-134). That is even more true of the south German cities. Of the approximately 65 imperial free cities, more than 50 adopted the Reformation, and in each case it was because of the demand of the citizens, who as a rule were struggling with the council and the patricians (cf. Bernd Moeller, *Imperial Cities and the Reformation: Three Essays*, trans. H. C. Erik Midelfort and Mark U. Edwards, Jr. [Philadelphia, 1972] and *Stadt and Kirche im 16. Jahrhundert* [Gütersloh, 1978]). This almost always began with the demand that an Evangelical preacher be called or that a cleric who had adopted the new faith be confirmed in his office, until the entire city—or at least an overwhelming majority—finally became Evangelical.

Even where the cities were under a Catholic sovereign, they occasionally knew how to push through the Reformation within their walls; Magdeburg and Halberstadt, for example, which were ruled by Albrecht of Mainz, were granted their request by their ecclesiastical overlord (who was continually in financial difficulties) after they paid an indemnity. Only where the pressure of the strong Catholic government was too intense could the formation of Evangelical congregations be prevented. In the moment when this pressure ceased or at least was reduced, we see them spontaneously springing up everywhere, for example, in Ducal Saxony and Brandenburg, even before the official promotion of the Reformation began.

## 5. DID THE REFORMATION DESTROY THE UNITY OF CHRISTIANITY?

Again and again, and in the most varied circumstances, one hears the claim that there was only one Christian church until the sixteenth century, and then the Reformation destroyed this unity of Christianity. This claim, convincing at first, is erroneous in many respects. In the first place, such a statement can apply to the unity of the church until 1517 only in the most limited sense. For the Christian church had already been divided for five hundred years before the Reformation, ever since the day when the papal legates laid the bull of excommunication upon the altar of the Hagia Sophia church in Constantinople. That happened on June 16, 1054. The attempts to bring the separated bodies together, which culminated in the Council of Florence in 1439, all came to nought. The gulf between the Eastern and Western churches had become so wide that not even a sincere effort could bridge it. In addition the tactically conditioned and politically influenced activity that we find in this and other conciliar attempts at union only aggravated the situation.

But one must go back even farther. This alleged unified church, which the Reformation is accused of splitting, was not first divided in the eleventh century, but in the fifth and sixth centuries. At that time, a thousand years before the Reformation began, a large number of eastern national churches separated from the universal church as a result of the Christological controversy. Today they have shrunk to a shadow of their former size and influence, but that does not change the fact that up to the Middle Ages they represented the form of Christianity that was found as far east as China.

The statement about church unity being destroyed by the Reformation at the beginning of the sixteenth century is only true when we observe the universal church under very limited conditions. Only when we look exclusively at the church in the West can it be true. It cannot easily be denied that in the West, church unity was preserved only with the aid of force. If the inquisition and the state had not exercised all their power, the rival churches of the Cathari and the Waldensians (to mention only two), instead of actually existing secretly, would certainly have played a similar impressive role in the waning Middle Ages that the rival churches of the Marcionites, the Novatians, and others played in the early church.

In addition, it is certain that in France the separation of the church from Rome was prevented only because in moving the papacy to Avignon France brought it under its power. During the schism the Avignon pope stood under the domination of France so there was no longer a necessity for the French to further what had already become a considerable separation from the universal church. In England the split of the church was only prevented by a for-

tunate political constellation that made it possible to per-
secute and eliminate Wycliffe's followers. In Bohemia it
was the disunity of the Hussites that finally allowed the
empire and church, after lengthy unsuccessful efforts, to
break the power of their previously invincible opponent and
prevent the splintering of the Bohemian church. Without
these events—here of necessity only briefly described—at
least a schism within the Catholic church would have occurred in France, England, and Bohemia, perhaps even an
actual secession of the entire church of these lands.

So much for the repeated accusation: "There was only one
Christian church until the sixteenth century, and then the
Reformation destroyed this unity of Christianity." Nevertheless, it is true that after the posting of Martin Luther's theses
on October 31, 1517, the proud structure of the western
church fell in ruins within a few years. Thousands of people
first in Germany, then in Switzerland, France, England,
and all of Europe, fell away from the church of the past
and became adherents of the new form of faith. All attempts
to prevent the spread of this new faith by the traditional
means of persecution and war were futile. In the Peace of
Augsburg in 1555 the existence of the new confession
had to be acknowledged legally even by its opponents. Even
where this official recognition of the new faith was successfully revoked for a time, it could be accomplished only
through bloody oppression. But the new faith could not be
stamped out. Even though it took a long time in some areas
(until the end of the eighteenth century in Austria and
France), it achieved legal recognition everywhere in Europe
after it had long since won a firm place in the consciousness
of the people.

# Abbreviations

*WA—D. Martin Luthers Werke,* 61 vols. (Weimar, 1883-).

*WA  TR—D. Martin Luthers Werke, Tischreden,* 6 vols. (Weimar, 1912-1921).

*WA  BR—D. Martin Luthers Werke, Briefwechsel,* 15 vols. (Weimar, 1883-).

*LW—Luther's Works,* ed. Jaroslav Pelikan and Helmut T. Lehmann, 56 vols. (St. Louis and Philadelphia, 1955-).

*S-J—Luther's Correspondence and Other Contemporary Letters,* ed. Preserved Smith and C. M. Jacobs, 2 vols. (Philadelphia, 1913-1918).

*CR—Corpus Reformatorum,* 100 vols. (Halle, Brunswick, and Leipzig, 1834-).

*SM—Supplementa Melanchthonia: Werke Philipp Melanchthon, die im Corpus Reformatorum vermisst werden,* 6 vols. (Leipzig, 1910).

*StA—Melanchthons Werke in Auswahl,* 8 vols. (Gütersloh, 1951-1971).

*OS—J. Calvini opera selecta,* ed. Peter Barth and Wilhelm Niesel, 6 vols. (Munich, 1926-1952).

Dillenberger—*John Calvin: Selections from His Writings,* ed. John Dillenberger (Garden City, N.Y., 1971).

*Letters—The Letters of John Calvin,* compiled Jules Bonnet, trans. Marcus Robert Gilchrist, 4 vols., reprint ed. (New York, 1972).

*SW—Ulrich Zwingli (1484-1531): Selected Works,* ed. Samuel Macauley Jackson, rev. ed. (Philadelphia, 1972).

*BK—Die Bekenntnisschriften der evangelisch-lutherischen Kirche,* 6th ed. (Göttingen, 1967).

*BC—The Book of Concord: The Confessions of The Evangelical Lutheran Church,* trans. and ed. Theodore G. Tappert et al. (Philadelphia, 1959).

# Notes

## Martin Luther

1. Julius Köstlin and Gustav Kawerau, *Martin Luther: Sein Leben und seine Schriften*, 2 vols., 3rd ed. (Berlin, 1905).
2. Otto Scheel, *Martin Luther*, 2 vols., 3rd and 4th eds. (Tübingen, 1920, 1930).
3. In 1899 Johannes Ficker discovered a copy of the lectures on Romans in the Vatican Library, but they were first published in 1908 (after Heinrich Denifle had included parts of them in his publications of 1903 and 1905). In the meantime it was learned that Luther's original manuscript was in the State Library in Berlin, had been described in the catalogue of manuscripts, and had even been displayed publicly in 1846, without being noticed by Luther scholars. In 1918 the first edition of the copies of the Galatians lectures by Hans von Schubert appeared, and in 1929 two editions of the lectures on Hebrews were published. The first lectures on the Psalms had been known for a long time, and had been published in the WA in 1885-1886.
4. *Luther: His Life and Times,* trans. John Nowell (New York, 1970).
5. *Luther: A Play* (London, 1961).
6. *Martin Luther & Thomas Münzer oder Die Einführung der Buchhaltung* (Berlin, 1971).
7. Cf. Kurt Aland, *Martin Luther in der modernen Literatur: Ein kritischer Dokumentarbericht* (Witten, 1973), pp. 369-397. This gives the most important portions of the text, but a complete critical edition is being planned.

8. "Deutschland und die Deutschen," *Gesammelte Werke*, ed. S. Fischer, 12 vols. (Oldenburg, 1960), 11:1126-1148.

9. "Die drei Gewaltigen," ibid., 10:374-383.

10. Cf. Aland, pp. 117-172, especially pp. 154-172.

11. Cf. ibid., pp. 19-87 (a critical analysis), and pp. 88-116 (a refutation of Forte's chief thesis).

12. Cf. *Das katholische Lutherbild im Bann der Lutherkommentare des Cochläus*, 3 vols. (Munster, 1943), vol. 1, p. ix.

13. Really Johannes Dobeneck (1479-1552). After studying at Cologne, Bologna, and Ferrara, he worked in Germany from 1519 on. In 1528 he became the court chaplain to Duke George of Saxony, and after 1539 was a canon in Breslau. He took part in all important religious discussions of the period, as early as 1521 acting as advisor to the papal nuncio Aleander at the Diet of Worms. He was the author of more than 200 writings, among which the most influential were his *Commentaria*.

14. These references to Engels' writing are from *The German Revolutions*, ed. Leonard Krieger (Chicago, 1967), pp. 39-43.

15. *Deutsche Geschichte vom Ausgang des Mittelalters*, numerous editions since 1910-1911.

16. *Der Kommunismus in der deutschen Reformation*, Vol. 2 of *Vorläufer des neuen Sozialismus*, 2nd ed. (Stuttgart, 1909), numerous later editions.

17. *Die Volksreformation des Thomas Müntzer und der grosse Bauernkrieg*, trans. H. Nichtweiss, 2nd ed. (Berlin, 1956).

18. Günther Wartenberg, "Bibliographie der marxistischen Luther-Literatur in der DDR, 1945-1966," *Luther-Jahrbuch*, 35 (1968):162-172. Cf. Hans-Gerhard Koch, *Luthers Reformation in kommunistischer Sicht* (Stuttgart, 1967).

19. At that time the first edition of his book, *Thomas Münzer als Theologe der Revolution*, appeared. The revision of 1960 had "a few factual corrections," but no changes in his position. The new edition of 1969 (Vol. 2 of his collected works) is only a reprint of the 1960 edition.

20. *WA TR* 3:415-416, Number 3566 (*LW* 54:234-235).

21. *WA TR* 2:134, Number 1559 (*LW* 54:157).

22. Cf. *WA TR* 4:440, Number 4707.

23. *CR* 6:158-159.

24. Cf. *WA TR* 4:303-304, Number 4414 (*LW* 54:337-338); *WA TR* 4:440, Number 4707; etc.

25. Cf. *WA TR* 1:294, Number 623 (*LW* 54:109); *WA TR* 1:439-440, Number 881; *WA* 44:711-712 (*LW* 8:181-182); etc.

26. *WA* 30³:530.

27. *WA* 38:143. Cf. Otto Scheel, *Dokumente zu Luthers Entwicklung*, 2nd ed. (Tübingen, 1929).

28. *WA* 1:557 (*LW* 31:129).

29. *WA* 54:185 (*LW* 34:336-337).

30. *WA* 54:186 (*LW* 34:336-337).

31. Cf. Otto Hermann Pesch, *Zur Frage nach Luthers reformatorischer Wende*, Vol. 123 of *Wege der Forschung*, (Darmstadt, 1968), pp. 445-505.

32. Heinrich Boehmer, *Road to Reformation*, trans. John W. Doberstein and Theodore G. Tappert (Philadelphia, 1946), pp. 118-163.

33. Gerhard Ebeling, *Luther: An Introduction to His Thought*, trans. R. A. Wilson (Philadelphia, 1970), p. 55. Ebeling, however, does not draw this conclusion, but is of the opinion that the tower experience should be dated in 1514.

34. *Quaestio de viribus et voluntate hominis sine gratia disputa*, *WA* 1:145-151; *WA* 9:768.

35. *Disputation Against Scholastic Theology* (September 4, 1517), *WA* 1:224-228 (*LW* 31:9-16); *WA* 9:768-769.

36. *WA* 1:353-374 (*LW* 31:39-70); *WA* 9:161-169.

37. *WA TR* 5:210, Number 5518 (*LW* 54:442-443).

38. *WA* 54:186 (*LW* 34:337).

39. *Against Hanswurst* (1541), *WA* 51:538 (*LW* 41:231).

40. There is no need here to go into the numerous articles on this much discussed subject. Cf. Erwin Iserloh, *The Theses Were Not Posted: Luther Between Reform and Reformation*, trans. Jared Wicks (Boston, 1968); and Klemens Honselmann, *Urfassung und Drucke der Ablassthesen Martin Luthers und ihre Veröffentlichung* (Paderborn, 1966). Representing the opposite view are Kurt Aland, *Martin Luther's 95 Theses: With the Pertinent Documents from the History of the Reformation*, trans. Ronald Diener (St. Louis, 1967), and Heinrich Bornkamm, *Thesen und Thesenanschlag Luthers: Geschehen und Bedeutung* (Berlin, 1967).

41. *WA* 54:179 (*LW* 34:328).

42. *WA TR* 1:601, Number 1206.

43. *WA BR* 1:110-112, Number 48 (*LW* 48:45-49).

44. *WA* 1:529.

45. "The trumpets of the new indulgence" are sounding, while Luther is still considering what "repentance" is. *WA* 1:525-526.

46. *Disputatio Johannis Eccii et Lutheri Lipsiae habita*, *WA* 2:254-383.

47. *WA BR* 1:359-360, Number 161.

48. *WA* 6:404-469 (*LW* 44:123-217).

49. *The Babylonian Captivity of the Church* (1520), *WA* 6:497-573 (*LW* 36:11-126).

50. *WA* 54:206-299 (*LW* 41:263-376).

51. This distinction is not considered sufficiently by the Catholic study of the subject, Remigius Bäumer, *Martin Luther und der Papst*, 2nd ed. (Münster, 1970). On this topic, cf. Ernst Bizer, *Luther und der Papst* (Munich, 1958).

52. Cf. the extensive collection of articles in *Der Reichstag zu Worms von 1521,* ed. Fritz Reuter (Worms, 1971).

53. Letter to Frederick the Wise (March 5, 1522) after his departure from the Wartburg, *WA BR* 2:454-457, Number 455 (*LW* 48:389-393).

54. Called Invocavit Sermons after the name of the Sunday on which the series began, *WA* 10³:1-64 (*LW* 51:70-100).

55. This is programmatically displayed in *Temporal Authority: To What Extent It Should Be Obeyed* (1523), *WA* 11:249-250 (*LW* 45:88-89).

56. This is programmatically displayed in the introduction to the *German Mass* (1526), *WA* 19:75 (*LW* 53:63-64).

57. Letter to Frederick the Wise (October 31, 1525), *WA BR* 3:594-596, Number 937.

58. *WA* 26:195-240 (*LW* 40:269-320).

59. *WA* 30¹:243-425 (426-474), 822-823 (*BK,* 501-541; *BC,* 338-356); *WA* 30¹:125-238 (*BK,* 545-733; *BC,* 358-461).

60. *WA* 18:62 (*LW* 40:79).

61. *WA* 18:76 (*LW* 40:92).

62. Romans 10:4.

63. *How Christians Should Regard Moses* (1525), *WA* 24:9 (*LW* 35:167).

64. *WA* 24:15 (*LW* 35:173).

65. The texts are given in Günther Franz, *Quellen zur Geschichte des Bauernkrieges* (Darmstadt, 1963), pp. 9-81.

66. *WA* 18:291-334 (*LW* 46:17-43).

67. *A Sincere Admonition by Martin Luther to All Christians to Guard Against Insurrection and Rebellion* (1522), *WA* 8:680 (*LW* 45:63).

68. Cf. *WA BR* 2:142-143, Number 312 (*LW* 54:167-169); *WA BR* 2:144-145, Number 313; *WA BR* 2:147, Number 315. Spalatin himself seems to have criticized Luther's position sharply.

69. *Verantwortung D. M. Luthers auf das Büchlein wider die räuberischen und mörderischen Bauern, getan am Pfingsttage im Jahre 1525, WA* 17¹:265-267; *An Open Letter on the Harsh Book Against the Peasants* (July, 1525), *WA* 18:384-401 (*LW* 46:63-85).

70. Luther expected that the end of the world was imminent.

71. Letter to Spalatin (June 16, 1525), *WA BR* 3:533, Number 892 (S-J 2:324).

72. The most that can be said is that he had sympathy for her because of her need and loneliness. (A Wittenberg student and son of a Nuremberg patrician, Jerome Baumgärtner, to whom Katie apparently had taken a fancy, was not able to obtain his family's permission to marry a former nun. In January, 1525, he entered into a marriage "appropriate to his status.")

73. "I hope to live a short time yet, to gratify my father, who asked me to marry and leave him descendants," wrote Luther to Amsdorf (June 21, 1525), *LW BR* 3:541, Number 900 (S-J, 2:329).

74. Not without reason this letter to Amsdorf just cited continues: "Moreover, I would confirm what I have taught by my example, for many are yet afraid even in the present great light of the gospel. God has willed and caused my act."

75. Cf. the letters which Luther wrote during the final weeks before his death. (Only a few of them are to Katie, since most of the time Luther was in Wittenberg.) The most important are found in *Luther deutsch: Die Werke Martin Luthers in neuer Auswahl für die Gegenwart,* ed. Kurt Aland, 10 vols. and 3 supplementary vols., 3rd and 4th eds., (Stuttgart and Göttingen, 1959-1969), 10:333-340 (*LW* 50:277-281, 286-287, 300, 301-304, 305-306, 311-313).

76. *Bondage of the Will* (1525), *WA* 18:600-787 (*LW* 33:3-295).

77. Letter to Spalatin (October 19, 1516), *WA BR* 1:70, Number 27 (*LW* 54:23-26).

78. *De libero arbitrio diatribe sive collatio* (an English translation is *Luther and Erasmus: Free Will and Salvation,* trans. and ed. E. Gordon Rupp, Vol. 17 of *The Library of Christian Classics* [Philadelphia, [1969], pp. 35-97).

79. *WA* 18:786 (*LW* 33:295).

80. *WA* 18:738 (*LW* 33:288).

81. *WA* 18:738 (*LW* 33:289).

82. *WA* 30³:276-320 (*LW* 47:11-55).

83. *WA* 30³:298-299 (*LW* 47:35).

84. *WA* 30³:277-278 (*LW* 47:13).

85. Quoted in the Formula of Concord, Solid Declaration, Article VII (*BK,* 976-978; *BC,* 571-572).

86. *WA* 30³:518-527 (*LW* 40:383-394). Cf. *That a Christian Assembly or Congregation Has the Right and Power to Judge All Teaching and to Call, Appoint, and Dismiss Teachers, Established and Proven by Scripture* (1523), *WA* 11:408-416 (*LW* 39:305-314), and *Concerning the Order of Public Worship* (1523), *WA* 12:35-37 (*LW* 53:11-14), and other writings from 1523.

87. On this extraordinarily complicated subject, cf. *Gesetz und Evangelium: Beiträge zur gegenwärtigen theologischen Diskussion,* ed. Ernst Kinder and Klaus Haendler, Vol. 142 of *Wege der Forschung* (Darmstadt, 1968), and the extensive bibliography given there.

88. *Against the Sabbatarians* (1538), *WA* 50:312-337 (*LW* 47:65-98); *Treatise on the Last Words of David* (1543), *WA* 54:28-100 (*LW* 15:267-352); *Vom Schem Hamphoras und vom Geschlecht Christi* (1543), *WA* 53:579-648; *On the Jews and Their Lies* (1543), *WA* 53:417-552 (*LW* 47:137-306).

89. *WA* 11:314-336 (*LW* 45:199-229).

90. Cf. *WA* 53:527 (*LW* 47:274).

91. *WA* 53:528 (*LW* 47:275).

92. *WA* 51:331-424. Cf. *Short Sermon on Usury* (1519), *WA* 6:3-8, *Long Sermon on Usury* (1520), *WA* 6:36-60 (*LW* 45:273-308), *Trade*

      and *Usury* (1524), *WA* 15:293-322 (*LW* 45:245-310), and a number of sermons.

93. *WA* 6:465 (*LW* 6:212).

94. Ed. Joachim Mehlhausen (Neukirchen, 1970).

95. The text is given in Karl Brandi, *Der Augsburger Religionsfriede vom 25. September 1555,* 2nd ed. (Göttingen, 1927).

96. *Huttens letzte Tage: Eine Dichtung,* "Luther," Section 32.

97. Even the title of this writing of 1554 expresses this: *De haereticis an sint persequendi, et omnino quomodo sit cum eis agendum, Luteri et Brentii, aliorumque tum veterum tum recentiorum sententiae,* facsimile ed. Sape van de Woude (Geneva, 1954). Its contents confirm this: 45 pages alone are devoted to reprinting Luther's *Temporal Authority: To What Extent It Should Be Obeyed.*

## Philip Melanchthon

1. Cf. below, pp. 126-129. It should be mentioned that all of the sections of this volume complement one another. This is especially true, for obvious reasons, of the chapters on Luther and Melanchthon.
2. *BK*, 10 (*BC*, 9-10).
3. *BK*, 10 (*BC*, 9).
4. *BK*, 9 (*BC*, 9).
5. *BK*, 50-83d (*BC*, 27-48).
6. *BK*, 84-137 (*BC*, 48-94).
7. This claim often appears in the literature, but it is correctly refuted by Wilhelm Maurer, *Der junge Melanchthon zwischen Humanismus und Reformation*, 2 vols. (Göttingen, 1967-1969), the pleasant sobriety of whose work supercedes the other modern Melanchthon biographies which, ever since Georg Ellinger, have often apologized for and glorified their subject and sometimes have assumed hagiographical character.
8. Mosellanus had already negotiated in Wittenberg and had declared himself ready to accept the call. Cf. Luther's letter to Spalatin (June 4, 1518), *WA BR* 1:180, Number 80.
9. The preface is in *CR* 1:14.
10. *Institutiones Graecae Grammaticae, CR* 1:24; *CR* 18:124; *CR* 20:3.
11. *Comoediae P. Terentii metro numerisque restitutae, CR* 19:655.
12. *Ex octavo convivialium quaestionum libro Plutarchi de nota Pathagorica, qua hospitium Hirundinem recipi nolebant. Phil. Melanchthone interprete, CR* 1:18; *CR* 17:1123-1137.
13. *Luciani Sophistae oratio in calumniam a Philippo Melanchthone latina facta, CR* 17:979-1145.

147

14. Cf. *CR* 1:9-13, 14, 18-20.
15. Cf. *CR* 1:16; *CR* 11:5; *StA* 3:17-28.
16. *CR* 1:6-7.
17. "At Deum immortalem, quam non spem de se praebet admodum etiam adolescens ac paene puer Ph. Melanchthon, utraque litteratura paena ex aequo suscipiendus. Quod inventionis acumen! Quae sermonis puritas et elegantia! Quanta reconditarum rerum memoria! quam varia lectio! quam verecundiae regiaeque prorsus indolis festivitas!" (Basel, 1516), p. 555.
18. Genesis 12:1-3.
19. *De corrigendis adolescentiae studiis, StA* 3:30-42.
20. *WA BR* 1:192, Number 88 (*LW* 48:78).
21. This is the way Melanchthon is occasionally described. Some of the contemporary graphics give an even more unfavorable impression. Yet the more renowned the artist, the more the spirituality animating his subject's face shines through. On the depicting of Melanchthon by contemporary and later artists, cf. Oskar Thulin, "Melanchthons Bildnis und Werk in zeitgenössischer Kunst," *Philipp Melanchthon: Forschungsbeiträge zur vierhundertsten Wiederkehr seines Todestages dargeboten in Wittenberg 1960,* ed. Walter Elliger (Göttingen, 1961), pp. 180-193, and Sibylle Harksen, "Bildnisse Philipp Melanchthons," *Philipp Melanchthon: Humanist, Reformator, Praeceptor Germaniae* (Berlin, 1963), pp. 270-287.
22. Beda Grundl, ed., "Achtzehn ungedruckte Briefe aus der Briefsammlung Veit Bilds," *Zeitschrift des Historischen Vereins für Schwaben und Neuburg,* 20 (1893) :221. Cf. Luther's letters to Spalatin (September 2, 1518), *WA BR* 1:196, Number 90 (*LW* 48:81-83), "His classroom is jammed with students," and (July 28, 1520), *WA BR* 2:149, Number 316, where about 500 students are mentioned.
23. *Urkundenbuch der Universität Wittenberg,* ed. Walter Friedensburg (Magdeburg, 1926-1927), 1:109.
24. *WA BR* 1:196, Number 90 (*LW* 48:83). Cf. Luther's letter to Lang (September 16, 1518), *WA BR* 1:203, Number 93 (S-J, 1:113), "He is a mere boy in years, but one of us in various knowledge, including that of almost all books."
25. *WA BR* 1:362, Number 163 (*LW* 48:119). This letter was apparently written under Melanchthon's influence, as was the one to Reuchlin (December 14, 1518), *WA BR* 1:268-269, Number 120 (S-J 1:138-139).
26. *WA BR* 1:212-213, Number 98 (S-J 1:118).
27. *WA BR* 1:252, Number 111 (S-J 1:131).
28. *WA BR* 12:12, Number 4213.
29. It appeared in print in October, 1518.
30. (October 11, 1518), *WA BR* 1:213, Number 98 (S-J 1:118).
31. Preface to the first volume of the Wittenberg edition of Luther's Latin writings, *WA* 54:179-187 (*LW* 34:327-338).

32. *WA* 54:182 (*LW* 34:331-332).

33. *Epistola de Lipsica disputatione* (1519), *CR* 1:87-96; *StA* 1:4-11 (S-J 1:200-202).

34. *Excusatio Eckii ad ea, quae falso sibi Phillippus Melanchthon Grammaticus Witenb. super Theologica Disputatione Lipsica adscripsit* (1519), *CR* 1:97-103.

35. *Defensio Philippi Melanchthonis contra Iohannem Eckium Theologiae Professorem* (1519), *CR* 1:108-118; *StA* 1:13-22.

36. *Oratio ad principes et populos Germaniae in Martinum Lutherum* (1520), *CR* 1:212-262.

37. *Th. Rhadini Todischi Placentini in M. Lutherum oratio.*

38. *Didymi Faventini adversus Thomam Placentinum Oratio pro Martino Luthero Theologo* (1521), *CR* 1:288-358; *StA* 1:57-140.

39. Didymus means "twin brother," which does not indicate, as Karl Sell supposed, the Apostle Thomas. Faventinus means "he who is favorably disposed (to Luther)." In addition, the concluding Greek sentence only very thinly conceals the name of Melanchthon by altering the order of the letters.

40. One in 1522 by Rhadino himself; one in 1534 by Cochlaeus.

41. *Determinatio Theologorum Parisiensium super doctrina Lutheriana, CR* 1:366-388.

42. *CR* 1:399-416; *StA* 1:142-162.

43. *CR* 1:318; *StA* 1:92-93.

44. *SM* 6:78-79, Number 1; *StA* 1:24-25.

45. Letter to Staupitz (October 3, 1519), *WA BR* 1:514, Number 202 (S-J 1:219-221).

46. Ibid.

47. He began his teaching activity in the winter semester of 1518 with lectures on Homer and the Epistle to Titus.

48. *Declamatiuncula in Divi Pauli doctrinam, CR* 1:136-146 (only the two prefaces); *StA* 1:27-53; the quotation is from *StA* 1:29.

49. The complete title is *Loci communes rerum theologicarum seu Hypotyposes theologicae, CR* 21:81-228; *StA* $2^1$:3-163. (An English translation of the 1521 edition by Lowell J. Satre is *Melanchthon and Bucer,* ed. Wilhelm Pauck, Vol. 19 of *The Library of Christian Classics* [Philadelphia, 1969], pp. 18-152).

50. Cf. below, pp. 97-99.

51. The title of the last edition to appear during his lifetime (1559) is characteristic: *Loci praecipui theologici, nunc denuo cura et diligentia summa recogniti, multisque in locis copiose illustrati, CR* 21, 601-1106; *StA* $2^1$:165-$2^2$:816. (An English translation of the 1555 edition is *Melanchthon on Christian Doctrine: Loci Communes, 1555,* trans. and ed. Clyde L. Manschreck [New York, 1965]).

52. Printing began in 1520, but was not completed until 1521. In a new edition in 1522 Melanchthon made changes, as he did in the numerous subsequent editions during his lifetime; for a time a new printing

came out almost every year. Thorough revisions took place in the editions of 1535 and 1544. For details, cf. Hans Engelland in *StA* 2$^1$:164-165.

53. *WA* 18:601 (*LW* 33:16).

54. Ibid.

55. Cf. Maurer, 2:51-54 and 2:64-67.

56. The impression that Thomas Blaurer formed about Melanchthon when he arrived in Wittenberg in 1521 is characteristic: "Phillipus, qui relictis humanis literis totus se dedidit christianis et sacris literis, ad quas et nos exhortatur, ut nullus prope sit Vittenberge, qui non biblia secum in manu circumferat, cepit me vel leviter amare. Lutherus psalmos praelegit, Philippus Paulum, alii alia; sed omnes coniurarunt in Lutherum atque adeo in Philippum ipsum." *Briefwechsel der Brüder Ambrosius und Thomas Blaurer, 1509-1548,* ed. Traugott Schiess, 3 vols. (Freiburg, 1908-1912), 1:30.

57. *WA BR* 2:574, Number 515.

58. *WA BR* 3:258-259, Number 723 (S-J 2:223-224).

59. The text is in *WA BR* 3:259.

60. The beginning of October, 1524, *CR* 1:677.

61. The end of September, 1522: "Nam theologica, quae praelegere coeperam propter Baccalaureatum, ut mos est, omittere malim," *CR* 1:575.

62. On this thesis which I first proposed in 1952, and on the Wittenberg theological faculty in general, cf. Kurt Aland, "Die Theologische Fakultät Wittenberg und ihre Stellung im Gesamtzusammenhang der Leucorea während des 16. Jahrhunderts," *Kirchengeschichtliche Entwürfe* (Gütersloh, 1960), pp. 283-394.

63. Cf. the summary of Melanchthon's positive judgments of Aristotle in Karl Hartfelder, *Philipp Melanchthon als Praeceptor Germaniae,* reprint ed. (Nieuwkoop, 1964), pp. 180-183.

64. Extensive discussions of this are found in the article referred to in note 62.

65. Yet Luther should not recede as far into the background as usually happens in the literature. Cf. Hermann Kunst, "Martin Luther und die Schule," *Dem Wort gehorsam: Landesbischof D. Hermann Dietzfelbinger D.D. zum 65. Geburtstag* (Munich, 1973), pp. 217-241.

66. *WA* 26:195-240 (*LW* 40:269-320). It must be mentioned, however, that Luther's contribution is greater than it appears to be at first sight (cf. *WA* 26:176). The preface of 1538, and the changes that Luther made in the text at that time, lead one to the assumption that he dealt with the *Instructions* as if they were his own work.

67. "Ego, cum decreverit princeps, etiamsi quid non probabo, tamen nihil seditiose faciam, sed vel tacebo, vel cedam, vel feram, quidquid accidet. Tuli etiam antea servitutem paene deformem, cum saepe Lutherus magis suae naturae, in qua *philoneikia* erat non exigua, quam vel personae suae, vel utilitati communi serviret," *CR* 6:880.

68. *CR* 6:882.
69. *CR* 41:593 *(Letters* 2:270-275).
70. *CR* 41:594 *(Letters* 2:271).
71. *CR* 41:594 *(Letters* 2:272).
72. *CR* 41:596.
73. Letter to Farel (March, 1539), *CR* 38:331 *(Letters* 1:130).
74. *BK,* 64-65 *(BC,* 34).
75. Letter to Farel (November 27, 1554), *CR* 43:321, one of many examples.
76. On the details, cf. the article referred to in note 62.
77. The same thing also happened at that time to the university at Frankfurt on the Oder and also to the university at Erfurt, whose history extended back into the fourteenth century.
78. *StA* 3:9.
79. *CR* 9:1098.
80. Cf. Carl Schmidt, *Philipp Melanchthon: Sein Leben und ausgewählte Schriften der Väter der lutherischen Kirche* (Elberfeld, 1861), pp. 664-665.

## Ulrich Zwingli

1. *CR* 88:88-136.
2. *CR* 88:197-209.
3. *CR* 88:458-465.
4. *WA* 1:525-622.
5. *CR* 89:14-457.
6. *CR* 88:458.
7. *CR* 88:466-468.
8. *CR* 89:144-150.
9. *CR* 89:217-222.
10. *De vera et falsa religione commentarius, CR* 90:590-912.
11. *CR* 88:458-459 (*SW*, 111).
12. *CR* 88:459 (*SW*, 112).
13. *CR* 88:460-461 (*SW*, 112-113).
14. *CR* 88:461-462 (*SW*, 113-114).
15. *CR* 88:463 (*SW*, 114-115).
16. *CR* 88:463-464 (*SW*, 115-117).
17. *CR* 88:464-465 (*SW*, 117).
18. *CR* 88:462-463 (*SW*, 114-115).
19. *CR* 88:465 (*SW*, 117).
20. *CR* 88:469-471.
21. *CR* 89:680-803.
22. This is shown indirectly by Zwingli's letter to Utinger (December 5, 1518), *CR* 94:110-113.
23. From the same letter, *CR* 94:111.
24. *CR* 94:112.

152

25. Cf. Oskar Vasella, *Reform und Reformation in der Schweiz: Zur Würdigung der Anfänge der Glaubenskrise,* 2nd ed. (Münster, 1965). It is noteworthy that this appeared as Vol. 16 of *Katholisches Leben und Kämpfen im Zeitalter der Glaubensspaltung: Vereinsschriften der Gesellschaft zur Herausgabe des Corpus Catholicorum.*

26. *CR* 94:112.

27. Letter to an unknown recipient, *CR* 95:677-678.

28. *Fidei christianae expositio.* Ulrich Zwingli, *Eine Auswahl aus seinen Schriften auf das vierhundertjährige Jubiläum der Züricher Reformation, im Auftrag des Kantons Zürich,* trans. and ed. Georg Finsler, Walther Köhler, and Arnold Rüegg (Zurich, 1918), p. 814.

29. The letter itself is not extant, but cf. the reply of Zasius (November 13, 1519) which refers to it, *CR* 94:222, and Zwingli's report to Myconius (January 4, 1520), *CR* 94:250-251.

30. Cf. the letters to Beatus Rhenanus (June 25, 1519), *CR* 94:190, and (July 2, 1519), *CR* 94:192.

31. Letter from Beatus Rhenanus (December 6, 1518), *CR* 94:114.

32. Cf. *CR* 89:145.

33. Obviously some time would have elapsed between its publication and Zwingli's reading of it.

34. *Auslegung und Gründe der Schlussreden* (Art. 21), *CR* 89:225.

35. *Huldrych Zwingli,* 2nd ed. (Stuttgart, 1952), p. 71.

36. The *Gebetslied in der Pest, CR* 88:67-69, was certainly not written during the illness itself, but after his recovery in 1520. It mirrors Zwingli's further development.

37. Cf. *CR* 89:147-150, as an example.

38. Examples are *CR* 94:485; *CR* 88:224; *CR* 88:256; *CR* 88:285; *CR* 89:3; *CR* 89:149. Cf. *CR* 92:613 and 712, which was, however, written as a direct polemic against Luther in the Sacramentarian Controversy.

39. *CR* 89:314.

40. Cf. Konrad Hofmann's complaint about this; a report concerning it is in Oskar Farner, *Huldrych Zwingli,* 4 vols. (Zurich, 1943-1960), 2:389-392. Zwingli expressed himself on this in *CR* 7:518. A survey of the most important early anti-Catholic sermons is in Farner, 3:119-129.

# John Calvin

1. *CR* 33:386; *OS* 1:458 (Dillenberger, 83).
2. *CR* 59:21/22 (Dillenberger, 26). Cf. below, p. 113. A parallel is the section defending his turning away from the Catholic church in *Reply to Sadolet, CR* 33:411-412; *OS* 1:484-485 (Dillenberger, 112) which without doubt has an autobiographical character. The objection raised, for example, by Fritz Büsser, *Calvins Urteil über sich selbst* (Zurich, 1950), pp. 30-31, that "Calvin's own experience" could not "at least partially lie behind this account" since "it would be difficult to identify him with the layman converted by this preacher," does not speak to the subject; the parallels to the preface to the Psalms commentary are too great. Rather, the two supplement one another in referring to the early period. In addition, Calvin has a "layman" speak because Sadolet also used a layman as his spokesman in this context.
3. One could compare this with Luther's preface to the first volume of the Wittenberg edition of his Latin writings in 1545. When one claims (as is frequently done in the literature on Calvin) that, in comparison with Calvin, Luther is very "talkative" about himself, one forgets that the major portion of these statements comes from the accounts of his Table Talk and not from Luther's writings themselves. It also overlooks the fact that Calvin frequently speaks about himself in his letters, e.g., about his illnesses, and is also "talkative."
4. *CR* 59:21/22 (Dillenberger, 26).
5. *CR* 59:21-23/22-24 (Dillenberger, 26-27). On this matter, recent literature is Fritz Büsser, *Calvins Urteil über sich selbst* (Zurich, 1950), and Paul Sprenger, *Das Rätsel um die Bekehrung Calvins*

154

(Neukirchen, 1960). Older literature is A. Lang, *Die Bekehrung Johannes Calvins* (Leipzig, 1897; reprint ed., Aalen, 1972); Karl Müller, "Calvins Bekehrung," *Nachrichten von der Königl. Gesellschaft der Wissenschaften zu Göttingen, philologisch-historische Klasse*, 1905, pp. 188-255; P. Wernle, "Noch einmal die Bekehrung Calvins," *Zeitschrift für Kirchengeschichte*, 27 (1906) :84-99; Karl Holl, *Johannes Calvin* (Tübingen, 1909 [*Gesammelte Aufsätze*, 3:254-284]); and P. Wernle, "Zu Calvins Bekehrung," *Zeitschrift für Kirchengeschichte*, 31 (1910) :556-583. We cannot here go into the extremely complicated discussion, which, in the amount and learnedness of the literature (and in their often methodologically incorrect beginnings) reminds one of the discussions concerning Luther's autobiographical retrospect of 1545; we can only attempt briefly to present our own position.

6. *CR* 33:411-412; *OS* 1:484-485 (Dillenberger, 112).
7. *CR* 33:412-413; *OS* 1:485-486 (Dillenberger, 113).
8. *CR* 33:413; *OS* 1:486 (Dillenberger, 114).
9. *CR* 59:23/26 (Dillenberger, 28).
10. Confession de la foy laquelle tous bourgeois et habitans de Geneve et subiects du pays doibvent iurer de garder et tenir. Extraicte de Linstruction dont on use en leglise de la dicte ville, *CR* 50:85-96; *OS* 1, 418-426.
11. Articles concernant l'organisation de l'église et du culte à Genève, proposés au Conseil par les ministres, *CR* 38:5-14; *OS* 1:369-377.
12. *CR* 38:15-30; *OS* 2:328-389 (abridged in Dillenberger, 229-244).
13. *CR* 38:121-122.
14. *CR* 42:606.
15. Letter to Farel and Viret (April, 1546), *CR* 40:335-336 *(Letters* 2:54).
16. Letter to Viret (August 11, 1546), *CR* 40:369.
17. *CR* 49:377.
18. Letter to Viret (July 2, 1546), *CR* 40:546 *(Letters* 2:123).
19. Letter to Viret (March 27, 1547), *CR* 40:505 *(Letters* 2:106-107).
20. Letter to Perrin (April, 1546), *CR* 40:338 *(Letters* 2:56-58).
21. Letter to a Bernese Pastor (February, 1537), *CR* 38:86 *(Letters* 1:47-50).
22. Letter to Farel (October 8, 1539), *CR* 38:396-400 *(Letters* 1:151-157).
23. Letter to Viret (Beginning of 1544), *CR* 39:688 *(Letters* 1:408).
24. Letter to Farel (May 31, 1544), *CR* 39:720-721 *(Letters* 1:416-421).
25. *De haereticis, an sint persequendi* (1554), facsimilie ed. Sape van de Woude (Geneva, 1954), published under the pseudonym of Martinus Bellius. Calvin categorized this writing as "stuffed full of atrocious blasphemies," Letter to the church of Poitiers (February 20, 1555), *CR* 43:441 *(Letters* 3:144).
26. All attributes come from the letter of the Genevan pastors to the Zurich pastors (November 14, 1551), *CR* 36:206-207 *(Letters* 2:322-325).

27. Letter to Fabri, undated and incomplete, but very likely associated with the report on Bolsec.
28. *Historie de la vie, moeurs, actes, doctrine, constance et mort de Jean Calvin, jadis ministre de Genève,* new ed. (Lyon, 1875).
29. Letter to de Falais (End of December, 1555), *CR* 42:449.
30. *CR* 44:12.
31. *De erroribus Trinitatis* and *Christianismi Restitutio.* These were published in direct opposition to Calvin's *Institutes;* in an appendix Servetus reprinted 32 letters which he had written in refutation to Calvin.
32. Letter to Frellon (February 13, 1546), *CR* 40:282 (*Letters* 2:31).
33. Letter to Farel (February 13, 1546), *CR* 40:283 (*Letters* 2:33).
34. Letter to Sulzer (September 9, 1553), *CR* 42:615 (*Letters* 2:428).
35. Letter to Farel (August 20, 1553), *CR* 42:590 (*Letters* 2:417). In case the accusation were proved false, he could expect the same punishment for himself.
36. September 22, 1553, *CR* 36:806.
37. Letter to Farel (August 20, 1553), *CR* 42:590 (*Letters* 2:417).
38. *Defensio orthodoxae fidei de sacra Trinitate, contra prodigiosos errores Michaeli Serveti Hispani: ubi ostenditur haereticos jure gladii coercendos esse et nominatim de homine hoc tam impio juste et merite sumptum Genevae fuisse supplicium.*
39. Cf. above, pp. 107-108.
40. Letter to Sulzer (September 9, 1553), *CR* 42:615 (*Letters* 2:428).
41. *CR* 33:433-460.
42. Cf. the letter to Farel (February 26, 1540), *CR* 39:24, as an example.
43. Cf. the letter to Melanchthon (April 21, 1544), *CR* 39:698, or the letter to Melanchthon (June 28, 1545), *CR* 40:98 (*Letters* 1:466-468) as examples.
44. Cf. the letter to the Montbéliard pastors (May 8, 1544), *CR* 39:705. Similar, but very much sharper, is the letter to Schenck (April 22, 1560), *CR* 46:62: The "Saxon theologians" are destroying the church "not only by foolish self-reliance, but also by excessive pride." They believe to be a faithful likeness of Luther, but they are "full of inflated arrogance" instead of the greatness of his spirit. Calvin must despise "their dishonest calumny, their pride, and their stinking conceited chatter." Similar (and even sharper) statements are found in many places.
45. Letter to Schalling (March 25, 1557), *CR* 44:430.
46. Even in the *Consensus Tigurinus* (Article 24) was stated: "It is ... senseless to imprison Christ in the bread or to bind him to it."
47. Preface to the Psalms (July 22, 1557).
48. *Adversus cuiusdam Sacramentarii falsam criminationem* (1555).
49. *Reply to Sadolet, CR* 33:391; *OS* 1:463 (Dillenberger, 89).

# Bibliography

The translator has supplemented the German bibliographies by adding English editions of the Reformers' writings. Where available, English translations of works in the original bibliographies have been cited.

# Martin Luther

## Editions

The definitive work is the so-called Weimar Edition (*D. Martin Luthers Werke,* Weimar, 1883—), which is divided into the following sections: *Schriften* ("writings"), *Briefwechsel* ("correspondence"), *Tischreden* ("Table Talk"), and *Deutsche Bibel* ("German Bible"). At present almost 100 vols. have appeared and only a few remain to come (portions of the *Deutsche Bibel,* the supplements to Vol. 55, the revisions of Vols. 3 and 4 containing the first lectures on the Psalms, and especially the indexes, which unfortunately were interrupted with the first fascicle of Vol. 58). A study edition is *Luthers Werke,* ed. Otto Clemen, 8 vols., 3rd and 6th eds. (Berlin, 1962-1968). An edition in modern German is *Luther Deutsch: Die Werke Martin Luthers in neuer Auswahl für die Gegenwart,* ed. Kurt Aland, 10 vols., 3rd and 4th eds. (Stuttgart and Göttingen, 1959-1969), which is supplemented by an index volume (1974) and a *Lutherlexicon* (1974). An important collection of sources is Otto Scheel, *Dokumente zu Luthers Entwicklung,* 2nd ed. (Tübingen, 1929). A survey of all Luther's writings, sermons, and letters, together with all the editions of Luther's works since the Reformation, is Kurt Aland, *Hilfsbuch zum Lutherstudium,* 3rd ed. (Witten, 1970). There are numerous one-volume editions, e.g., Karl Gerhard Steck, *Martin Luther Studienausgabe* (Frankfurt, 1970), and Herman Kunst, *Martin Luther und die Kirche* (Stuttgart, 1971).

## English Editions

*Luther's Works.* Edited by Jaroslav Pelikan and Helmut T. Lehmann. 56 vols. to date. St. Louis and Philadelphia, 1955—.

159

*Works of Martin Luther.* Edited by Henry Eyster Jacobs. 6 vols. Philadelphia, 1915-1943.

*Reformation Writings of Martin Luther.* Translated and edited by Bertram Lee Woolf. 2 vols. New York, 1953-1956.

*Luther's Correspondence and Other Contemporary Letters.* Translated and edited by Preserved Smith and C. M. Jacobs. 2 vols. Philadelphia, 1913-1918.

*Luther: Lectures on Romans.* Translated and edited by Wilhelm Pauck. The Library of Christian Classics, vol. 15. Philadelphia, 1961.

*Luther: Early Theological Works.* Translated and edited by James Atkinson. The Library of Christian Classics, vol. 16. Philadelphia, 1955.

*Luther and Erasmus: Free Will and Salvation.* Translated and edited by E. Gordon Rupp and Philip S. Watson. The Library of Christian Classics, vol. 17. Philadelphia, 1969.

*Luther: Letters of Spiritual Counsel.* Edited by Theodore G. Tappert. The Library of Christian Classics, vol. 18. Philadelphia, 1955.

*Martin Luther: Selections from His Writings.* Edited by John Dillenberger. Chicago, 1961.

*Readings in Luther for Laymen.* Edited by Charles S. Anderson. Minneapolis, 1967.

### Bibliographies and Surveys of Research

Schottenloher, Karl. *Bibliographie zur deutschen Geschichte im Zeitalter der Glaubensspaltung 1517-1585.* 7 vols. Stuttgart, 1933-1966 (Includes literature through 1960.)

International Committee of Historical Sciences. *Bibliographie de la Réforme 1450-1648: Ouvrages parus de 1940 à 1955.* 8 vols. to date. Leiden, 1961—. (Organized according to countries and alphabetically arranged by author.)

*Lutherjahrbuch: Organ der internationalen Lutherforschung.* (Contains a continuing bibliography.)

*Archiv für Reformationsgeschichte* [Archive for Reformation History: An International Journal concerned with the history of the Reformation and its significance in world affairs]. (Contains a continuing bibliography.)

Asheim, Ivar, ed. *The Church, Mysticism, Sanctification, and the Natural in Luther's Thought: Lectures Presented to the Third International Congress on Luther Research.* Philadelphia, 1967.

Boehmer, Heinrich. *Luther and the Reformation in the Light of Modern Research.* London, 1930.

Kinder, Ernst, and Haendler, Klaus. *Gesetz und Evangelium: Beiträge zur gegenwärtigen theologischen Diskussion.* Wege der Forschung, vol. 142. Darmstadt, 1968.

Lohse, Bernard, ed. *Der Durchbruch der reformatorischen Erkenntnis bei Luther.* Wege der Forschung, vol. 123. Darmstadt, 1968.

Schrey, Heinz Horst. *Reich Gottes und Welt: Die Lehre Luthers von den zwei Reichen.* Wege der Forschung, vol. 107. Darmstadt, 1969.

Vajta, Vilmos, ed. *Lutherforschung heute: Referate und Berichte der ersten Internationalen Lutherforschungskongresses.* Berlin, 1958.

———. *Luther and Melanchthon in the History and Theology of the Reformation.* Philadelphia, 1961.

Wolf, Günter, ed. *Luther und die Obrigkeit.* Wege der Forschung, vol. 85. Darmstadt, 1972.

Wolff, Otto. *Die Haupttypen der neuen Lutherdeutung.* Stuttgart, 1938.

## Biographies

Bainton, Roland, H. *Here I Stand: A Life of Martin Luther.* New York, 1950.

Boehmer, Heinrich. *Road to Reformation.* Translated by John W. Doberstein and Theodore G. Tappert. Philadelphia, 1946.

Fausel, Heinrich. *D. Martin Luther: Der Reformator im Kampf um Evangelium und Kirche.* 2nd ed. Stuttgart, 1955.

Kawerau, Peter. *Luther: Leben, Schriften, Denken.* Marburg, 1969.

Köstlin, Julius, and Kawerau, Gustav. *Martin Luther: Sein Leben und seine Schriften.* 2 vols. 5th ed. Berlin, 1903.

Lau, Franz. *Luther.* Translated by Robert H. Fischer. Philadelphia, 1963.

Ritter, Gerhard. *Luther: His Life and Work.* Translated by John Riches. New York, 1963.

Scheel, Otto. *Martin Luther: Vom Katholizismus zur Reformation.* 2 vols. 3rd and 4th eds. Tübingen, 1921-1930.

## Monographs

Aland, Kurt. *Der Weg zur Reformation: Zeitpunkt und Charakter des reformatorischen Erlebnisses Martin Luthers.* Munich, 1965.

———. *Martin Luther in der modernen Literatur: Ein kritischer Dokumentarbericht.* Witten, 1973.

Althaus, Paul. *The Ethics of Martin Luther.* Translated by Robert C. Schultz. Philadelphia, 1972.

———. *The Theology of Martin Luther.* Translated by Robert C. Schultz. Philadelphia, 1966.

Asendorf, Ulrich. *Eschatologie bei Luther.* Göttingen, 1967.

Bandt, Hellmut. *Luthers Lehre vom verborgenen Gott: Eine Untersuchung zu dem offenbarungsgeschichtlichen Ansatz seiner Theologie.* Berlin, 1958.

Bayer, Oswald. *Promissio: Geschichte der reformatorischen Wende in Luthers Theologie.* Göttingen, 1971.

Beintker, Horst. *Die Überwindung der Anfechtung bei Luther: Eine Studie zu seiner Theologie nach den Operationes in Psalmos 1519-21.* Berlin, 1954.

Bizer, Ernst. *Fides ex auditu: Eine Untersuchung über die Entdeckung der Gerechtigkeit Gottes durch Martin Luther.* 4th ed. Neukirchen, 1964.

Bogdahn, Martin. *Die Rechtfertigungslehre Luthers im Urteil der neueren katholischen Theologie: Möglichkeiten und Tendenzen der katholischen Lutherdeutung in evangelischer Sicht.* Göttingen, 1971.

Bornkamm, Heinrich. *Das Jahrhundert der Reformation: Gestalten und Kräfte.* Göttingen, 1966.

———. *Luther and the Old Testament.* Translated by Eric W. and Ruth C. Gritsch. Philadelphia, 1969.

———. *Luther: Gestalt und Wirkungen.* Gütersloh, 1975.

———. *Luther im Spiegel der deutschen Geistesgeschichte.* 2nd ed. Göttingen, 1970.

———. *Luther's Doctrine of the Two Kingdoms in the Context of his Theology.* Translated by Karl H. Hertz. Philadelphia, 1966.

Bornkamm, Karin. *Luthers Auslegung des Galaterbriefes von 1519 und 1531: Ein Vergleich.* Berlin, 1963.

Brandenburg, Albert. *Gericht und Evangelium: Zur Worttheologie in Luthers erster Psalmenvorlesung.* Paderborn, 1960.

Brinkel, Karl. *Die Lehre Luthers von der fides infantium bei der Kindertaufe.* Berlin, 1958.

Dickens, A. G. *The German Nation and Martin Luther.* London, 1974.

Dörries, Hermann. *Beiträge zum Verständnis Luthers.* Wort und Stunde, vol. 3. Göttingen, 1970.

Ebeling, Gerhard. *Evangelische Evangelienauslegung: Eine Untersuchung zu Luthers Hermeneutik.* 2nd ed. Darmstadt, 1962.

———. *Luther: An Introduction to His Thought.* Translated by R. A. Wilson. Philadelphia, 1970.

———. *Lutherstudien.* Vol. 1. Tübingen, 1971.

Ferel, Martin. *Gepredigte Taufe: Eine homiletische Untersuchung zur Taufpredigt bei Luther.* Tübingen, 1969.

Götze, Ruth. *Wie Luther Kirchenzucht übte: Eine kritische Untersuchung von Luthers Bannsprüchen und ihrer exegetischer Grundlegung aus der Sicht unserer Zeit.* Berlin, 1959.

Hasler, August. *Luther in der katholischen Dogmatik: Darstellung seiner Rechtfertigungslehre in den katholischen Dogmatikbüchern.* Munich, 1968.

Heckel, Johannes. *Lex charitatis: Eine juristische Untersuchung über das Recht in der Theologie Martin Luthers.* 2nd ed. Cologne, 1973.

Heintze, Gerhard. *Luthers Predigt von Gesetz und Evangelium.* Munich, 1958.

Hermann, Rudolf. *Gesammelte Studien zur Theologie Luthers und der Reformation.* Göttingen, 1960.

———. *Luthers Theologie.* Gesammelte und nachgelassene Werke, vol. 1. Göttingen, 1967.

Hillerdahl, Gunnar. *Gehorsam gegen Gott und Menschen: Luthers Lehre von der Obrigkeit und die moderne evangelische Staatsethik.* Göttingen, 1955.

Hinrichs, Carl. *Luther und Müntzer.* 2nd ed. Berlin, 1971.

Hirsch, Emanuel. *Lutherstudien.* 2 vols. Gütersloh, 1954.

Holl, Karl. *Luther.* Gesammelte Aufsätze zur Kirchengeschichte, vol. 1. Reprint ed. Darmstadt, 1965.

————. *The Cultural Significance of the Reformation.* Translated by Karl and Barbara Hertz and John H. Lichtblau. New York, 1959.

————. *What did Luther Understand by Religion?* Edited by James Luther Adams and Walter F. Bense, translated by Fred W. Meuser and Walter R. Wietzke. Philadelphia, 1977.

Iserloh, Ernst. *Luther und die Reformation: Beiträge zu einem ökumenischen Lutherverständnis.* Aschaffenburg, 1974.

Iwand, Hans Joachim. *Glaubensgerechtigkeit nach Luthers Lehre.* 4th ed. Munich, 1964.

————. *Luthers Theologie.* Nachgelassene Werke, vol. 5. Munich, 1974.

————. *Rechtfertigungslehre und Christusglaube: Eine Untersuchung zur Systematik der Rechtfertigungslehre Luthers in ihren Anfängen.* Reprint ed. Munich, 1966.

Jetter, Werner. *Die Taufe beim jungen Luther: Eine Untersuchung über das Werden der reformatorischen Sakraments- und Taufanschauung.* Tübingen, 1954.

Kantzenbach, Friedrich Wilhelm. *Die Reformation in Deutschland und Europa.* Gütersloh, 1965.

————. *Martin Luther und die Anfänge der Reformation.* Gütersloh, 1965.

Kerlen, Dietrich. *Assertio: Die Entwicklung von Luthers theologischem Anspruch und der Streit mit Erasmus von Rotterdam.* Wiesbaden, 1976.

Kohls, Ernst-Wilhelm. *Luther oder Erasmus: Luthers Theologie in der Auseinandersetzung mit Erasmus.* Basel, 1973.

Koopmans, Jan. *Het oudkerkelijk dogma in de Reformatie, bepaaldelijk bij Calvijn.* Wageningen, 1938.

Kunst, Hermann. *Evangelischer Glaube und politische Verantwortung: Martin Luther als politischer Berater seines Landesherrn und seine Teilnahme an den Fragen des öffentlichen Lebens.* Stuttgart, 1977.

————. *Martin Luther und der Krieg: Eine kritische Betrachtung.* Stuttgart, 1968.

Lau, Franz. *Luthers Lehre von den beiden Reichen.* Berlin, 1952.

Link, Wilhelm. *Das Ringen Luthers um die Freiheit der Theologie von der Philosophie.* 2nd ed. Munich, 1955.

Loewenich, Walter von. *Luther als Ausleger der Synoptiker.* Munich, 1954.

————. *Luther und der Neuprotestantismus.* Witten, 1963.

————. *Luther's Theology of the Cross.* Translated by Herbert J. A. Bouman. Minneapolis, 1976.

Löfgren, David, *Die Theologie der Schöpfung bei Luther.* Göttingen, 1960.

Lohse, Bernhard. *Mönchtum und Reformation: Luthers Auseinander-setzung mit dem Mönchsideal des Mittelalters.* Göttingen, 1963.
————. *Ratio und Fides: Eine Untersuchung über die ratio in der Theologie Luthers.* Göttingen, 1957.
Mauser, Ulrich W. *Der junge Luther und die Häresie.* Gütersloh, 1968.
Meyer, Hans Bernhard. *Luther und die Messe: Eine liturgiewissenschaft-liche Untersuchung über das Verhältnis Luthers zum Messwesen des späten Mittelalters.* Paderborn, 1965.
Mülhaupt, Erwin. *Luther über Müntzer: Erläutert und an Thomas Münt-zers Schrifttum nachgeprüft.* Witten, 1973.
Schwarz, Reinhard. *Fides, spes und caritas beim jungen Luther.* Berlin, 1962.
Seils, Martin. *Der Gedanke vom Zusammenwirken Gottes und des Menschen in Luthers Theologie.* Gütersloh, 1962.
Stauffer, Richard. *Luther as Seen by Catholics.* Translated by Mary Parker and T. H. L. Parker. Richmond, Va., 1967.
Steck, Karl Gerhard. *Lehre und Kirche bei Luther.* Munich, 1963.
————. *Luther und die Schwärmer.* Zollikon, 1955.
Stein, Wolfgang. *Das kirchliche Amt bei Luther.* Wiesbaden, 1974.
Stephan, Horst. *Luther in den Wandlungen seiner Kirche.* 2nd ed. Berlin, 1951.
Tecklenburg-Johns, Christa. *Luthers Konzilsidee in ihrer historischen Bedingtheit und ihrem reformatorischen Neuansatz.* Berlin, 1966.
Trüdinger, Karl. *Luthers Briefe und Gutachten an weltliche Obrigkeiten zur Durchführung der Reformation.* Münster, 1975.
Vajta, Vilmos. *Luther on Worship: An Interpretation.* Translated by U. S. Leupold. Philadelphia, 1958.
Wingren, Gustav. *Luther on Vocation.* Translated by Carl C. Rasmussen. Philadelphia, 1957.
Wolf, Ernst. *Peregrinatio.* 2 vols. Munich, 1962-1965.
Wolf, Gerhard Philipp. *Das neuere französische Lutherbild.* Wiesbaden, 1974.
Zur Mühlen, Karl-Heinz. *Nos extra nos: Luthers Theologie zwischen Mystik und Scholastik.* Tübingen, 1972.

# Philip Melanchthon

### Editions

*Philippi Melanthonis Opera quae supersunt omnia.* Edited by C. G. Bretschneider and H. E. Bindseil. Corpus Reformatorum, vols. 1-28. Halle, 1834-1860.

*Ph. Melanchthonis Epistolae, iudicia, consilia, testimonia aliorumque ad eum epistolae quae in Corpore Reformatorum desiderantur.* Edited by H. E. Bindseil. Halle, 1874.

*Melanchthons Werke in Auswahl.* Edited by Robert Stupperich. 8 vols. to date. Gütersloh, 1951-1975.

*Texte aus der Anfangszeit Melanchthons.* Edited by Ernst Bizer. Neukirchen, 1961.

A chronological list of works is in Karl Hartfelder, *Philipp Melanchthon als Praeceptor Germaniae,* reprint ed. (Nieuwkoop, 1964), pp. 579-620.

### English Editions

*The Loci Communes of Philip Melanchthon.* Translated and edited by Charles L. Hill. Boston, 1944.

*Melanchthon and Bucer.* Edited by Wilhelm Pauck. The Library of Christian Classics, vol. 19. Philadelphia, 1969.

*Melanchthon on Christian Doctrine: Loci Communes 1555.* Translated and edited by Clyde L. Manschreck. New York, 1965.

*Melanchthon: Selected Writings.* Translated by Charles L. Hill, edited by Elmer E. Flack and Lowell J. Satre. Minneapolis, 1962.

### Bibliographies and Surveys of Research

For Schottenloher and the *Bibliographie de la Réforme,* see above under Luther, p. 160. A survey of older literature is also in Hartfelder, op. cit., pp. 621-645.

Elliger, Walter, ed. *Philipp Melanchthon: Forschungsbeiträge zur vierhundersten Wiederkehr seines Todestages dargeboten in Wittenberg 1960.* Göttingen, 1961.

Fraenkel, Peter, and Greschat, Martin. *Zwanzig Jahre Melanchthonstudium: Sechs Literaturberichte (1945-1965).* Geneva, 1967.

Hammer, Wilhelm. *Die Melanchthonforschung im Wandel der Jahrhunderte: Ein beschreibendes Verzeichnis.* 2 vols. Gütersloh, 1967-1968. (Vol. 1: 1519-1799; Vol. 2: 1800-1965.)

*Philipp Melanchthon: Humanist, Reformator, Praeceptor Germaniae.* Berlin, 1963.

### Biographies

Ellinger, Georg. *Philipp Melanchthon: Ein Lebensbild.* Berlin, 1902.

Hartfelder, Karl. *Philipp Melanchthon als Praeceptor Germaniae.* Reprint ed. Nieuwkoop, 1964.

Kooiman, W. J. *Philippus Melanchthon.* Amsterdam, 1963.

Manschreck, Clyde L. *Melanchthon: The Quiet Reformer.* New York, 1958.

Meinhold, Peter. *Philipp Melanchthon: Der Lehrer der Kirche.* Berlin, 1960.

Schmidt, Carl. *Philipp Melanchthon: Sein Leben und ausgewählte Schriften der Väter der lutherischen Kirche.* Elberfeld, 1861.

Stupperich, Robert. *Melanchthon.* Translated by Robert H. Fischer. Philadelphia, 1965.

### Monographs

Bizer, Ernst. *Theologie der Verheissung: Studien zur theologischen Entwicklung des jungen Melanchthon (1519-1524).* Neukirchen, 1964.

Brüls, Alfons. *Die Entwicklung der Gotteslehre beim jungen Melanchthon, 1518-1535.* Witten, 1975.

Engelland, Hans. *Melanchthon: Glauben und Handeln.* Munich, 1931.

Fraenkel, Peter. *Testimonia Patrum: The Function of the Patristic Argument in the Theology of Philipp Melanchthon.* Geneva, 1961.

Geyer, Hans-Georg. *Von der Geburt des wahren Menschen: Probleme aus den Anfängen der Theologie Melanchthons.* Neukirchen, 1965.

Greschat, Martin. *Melanchthon neben Luther: Studien zur Gestalt der Rechtfertigungslehre zwischen 1528 und 1537.* Witten, 1965.

Haendler, Klaus. *Wort und Glaube bei Melanchthon: Eine Untersuchung über die Voraussetzungen und Grundlagen des melanchthonischen Kirchenbegriffs.* Gütersloh, 1968.

Hübner, Friedrich. *Natürliche Theologie und theokratische Schwärmerei bei Melanchthon.* Gütersloh, 1936.

Huschke, Rolf Bernhard. *Melanchthons Lehre vom ordo politicus: Ein Beitrag zum Verhältnis von Glauben und politischem Handeln bei Melanchthon.* Gütersloh, 1968.

Kisch, Guido. *Melanchthons Rechts- und Soziallehre.* Berlin, 1967.

Maurer, Wilhelm. *Der junge Melanchthon zwischen Humanismus und Reformation.* 2 vols. Göttingen, 1967-1969.

————. *Melanchthon-Studien.* Gütersloh, 1964.

Neuser, Wilhelm H. *Der Ansatz der Theologie Melanchthons.* Neukirchen, 1957.

————. *Die Abendmahlslehre Melanchthons in ihrer geschichtlichen Entwicklung (1519-1530).* Neukirchen, 1968.

Nürnberger, Richard. *Kirche und weltliche Obrigkeit bei Melanchthon.* Würzburg, 1937.

Pfister, Hermann. *Die Entwicklung der Theologie Melanchthons unter dem Einfluss der Auseinandersetzung mit Schwarmgeistern und Wiedertäufern.* Freiburg, 1968.

Schäfer, Rolf. *Christologie und Sittlichkeit in Melanchthon frühen Loci.* Tübingen, 1961.

Schirmer, Arno. *Das Paulusverständnis Melanchthons 1518-1522.* Wiesbaden, 1967.

Schnell, Uwe. *Die homiletische Theorie Melanchthons.* Berlin, 1968.

Schwarzenau, Paul. *Der Wandel im theologischen Ansatz bei Melanchthon von 1525-1535.* Gütersloh, 1956.

Sick, Hansjörg. *Melanchthon als Ausleger des Alten Testaments.* Tübingen, 1959.

Sperl, Adolf. *Melanchthon zwischen Humanismus und Reformation: Eine Untersuchung über den Wandel des Traditionsverständnis bei Melanchthon und die damit zusammenhängenden Grundfragen seiner Theologie.* Munich, 1959.

Stupperich, Robert. *Der unbekannte Melanchthon: Wirken und Denken des Praeceptor Germaniae in neuer Sicht.* Stuttgart, 1961.

Weber, Gottfried. *Grundlagen und Normen politischer Ethik bei Melanchthon.* Munich, 1962.

Wolf, Ernst. *Philipp Melanchthon: Evangelischer Humanismus.* Göttingen, 1961.

# Ulrich Zwingli

### Editions

*Huldreich Zwingli: Sämtliche Werke.* Edited by E. Egli et al. Corpus Reformatorum, vols. 88-100. Berlin, 1905—; Leipzig, 1908—; and Zurich, 1959—. (To date Vols. 1-11 and 13-14 have appeared.)

*Zwingli: Hauptschriften.* Edited by Fritz Blanke, Rudolf Pfister, and Oskar Farner. 8 vols. to date. Zurich, 1940—.

*Ulrich Zwingli: Eine Auswahl aus seinen Schriften auf das vierhundert-jährige Jubiläum der Züricher Reformation, im Auftrage des Kantons Zürich.* Translated and edited by Georg Finsler. Zurich, 1918.

*Huldreich Zwingli: Auswahl seiner Schriften.* Edited by Edwin Künzli. Zurich, 1962.

Köhler, Walter. *Das Buch der Reformation Huldrych Zwinglis.* Munich, 1926. (A collection of texts.)

### English Editions

*Zwingli and Bullinger.* Translated by G. W. Bromily. The Library of Christian Classics, vol. 24. Philadelphia, 1953.

*Ulrich Zwingli (1484-1531): Selected Works.* Edited by Samuel Macauley Jackson. Revised ed. Philadelphia, 1972.

### Surveys of Research

Büsser, Fritz. *Das katholische Zwinglibild: Von der Reformation bis zur Gegenwart.* Zurich, 1968.

Finsler, Georg. *Zwingli-Bibliographie.* Reprint ed. Nieuwkoop, 1962. (For the period until 1897.)

Gäbler, Ulrich, "Die Zwingli-Forschung seit 1960," *Theologische Literaturzeitung,* 96 (1971): 482-490. (References to earlier literature are on p. 488.)

————. *Huldrych Zwingli im 20. Jahrhundert: Forschungsbericht und annotierte Bibliographie 1897-1972.* Zurich, 1975.

Guggisberg, Kurt. *Das Zwinglibild des Protestantismus im Wandel der Zeiten.* Leipzig, 1934.

Neuser, Wilhelm H., ed. *Calvinus Theologus: Die Referate Europäischen Kongresses für Calvinforschung vom 16. bis 19. September 1974 in Amsterdam.* Neukirchen, 1976.


**Periodical**

*Zwingliana: Mitteilungen zur Geschichte Zwinglis und der Reformation.* Zurich, 1904—.


**Biographies**

Büsser, Fritz. *Huldrych Zwingli: Reformation als prophetischer Auftrag.* Göttingen, 1973.

Courvoisier, Jacques. *Zwingli: A Reformed Theologian.* Richmond, Va., 1963.

Farner, Oskar. *Huldrych Zwingli.* 4 vols. Zurich, 1943-1960.

Haas, Martin. *Zwingli und seine Zeit: Leben und Werk des Züricher Reformators.* 2nd ed. Zurich, 1977.

Köhler, Walter. *Huldrych Zwingli.* 2nd ed. Stuttgart, 1952.

Schmidt-Clausing, Fritz. *Zwingli.* Berlin, 1965.

Staehelin, Rudolf. *Huldreich Zwingli: Sein Leben und Wirken nach den Quellen dargestellt.* 2 vols. Basel, 1895-1897.


**Monographs**

Farner, Alfred. *Die Lehre von Kirche und Staat bei Zwingli.* Tübingen, 1930.

Gestrich, Christof. *Zwingli als Theologe: Glaube und Geist beim Züricher Reformator.* Zurich, 1967.

Köhler, Walter. *Zwingli und Luther: Der Streit über das Abendmahl nach seinen politischen und religiösen Beziehungen.* 2 vols. Leipzig and Gütersloh, 1924-1953.

Kreutzer, Jakob. *Zwinglis Lehre von der Obrigkeit.* Reprint ed. Stuttgart, 1965.

Ley, Roger. *Kirchenzucht bei Zwingli.* Zurich, 1948.

Locher, Gottfried Wilhelm. *Die Theologie Huldrych Zwinglis im Lichte seiner Christologie.* Vol. 1. Zurich, 1952.

————. *Huldrych Zwingli in neuer Sicht: 10 Beiträge zur Theologie der Züricher Reformation.* Zurich, 1969.

Neuser, Wilhelm H. *Die reformatorische Wende bei Zwingli*. Neukirchen, 1978.

Rich, Arthur. *Die Anfänge der Theologie Huldrych Zwinglis*. Zurich, 1949.

Rogge, Joachim. *Zwingli und Erasmus: Die Friedensgedanken des jungen Zwingli*. Stuttgart, 1962.

Rother, Siegfried. *Die religiösen und geistigen Grundlagen der Politik Huldrych Zwinglis: Ein Beitrag zum Problem des christlichen Staates*. Erlangen, 1956.

Schmid, Heinrich. *Zwinglis Lehre von der göttlichen und menschlichen Gerechtigkeit*. Zurich, 1959.

# John Calvin

## Editions

*Johannis Calvini opera quae supersunt omnia.* Edited by G. Baum, E. Cunitz, and E. Reuss. Corpus Reformatorum, vols. 29-87. Brunswick, 1869-1900.

*Supplementa Calviniana (Sermons inédits).* 4 vols. to date. Neukirchen, 1936-1971. (A supplement to the preceding.)

*Opera selecta.* Edited by Peter Barth and Wilhelm Niesel. 5 vols. Reprint ed. Munich, 1963.

*Johannes Calvins Lebenswerk in seinen Briefen.* Edited by Rudolf Schwarz. 3 vols. 2nd ed. Neukirchen, 1961-1962.

*Unterricht in der christlichen Religion.* Edited by Otto Weber. 2nd ed. Neukirchen, 1963.

*Auslegung der heiligen Schrift.* Edited by E. F. K. Müller and Otto Weber. Old series. 14 vols. Neukirchen, n.d.

*Auslegung der heiligen Schrift.* Edited by Otto Weber et al. New Series. 9 vols. to date. Neukirchen, 1937-1966.

*Um Gottes Ehre! Vier kleinere Schriften Calvins.* Edited by Matthias Simon. Munich, 1924.

*Christliche Unterweisung: Der Genfer Katechismus von 1537.* Translated by Lothar Schuckert. Hamburg, 1963.

Smidt, U. *Calvin und die Kirche.* Stuttgart, 1972.

Neuser, Wilhelm H. Calvin. Kirchengeschichtliche Quellenhefte, vol. 14 Gladbeck, 1964.

171

**English Editions**

*John Calvin: Institutes of the Christian Religion.* Edited by John T. Mc-
Neill, translated by Ford L. Battles. 2 vols. The Library of Christian
Classics, vols. 20-21. Philadelphia, 1960.

*Calvin: Theological Treatises.* Translated by J. K. S. Reid. The Library
of Christian Classics, vol. 22. Philadelphia, 1954.

*Calvin: Commentaries.* Translated and edited by Joseph Haroutunian and
Louise Pettibone Smith. The Library of Christian Classics, vol. 23.
Philadelphia, 1958.

*Calvin's Tracts and Treatises.* Translated by Henry Beveridge. 3 vols.
Reprint ed. Grand Rapids, 1958.

*The Letters of John Calvin.* Compiled by Jules Bonnet, translated by
Marcus Robert Gilcrist. 4 vols. Reprint ed. New York, 1972.

*Commentaries of John Calvin.* 46 vols. Reprint ed. Grand Rapids, 1959-1972.

*Instruction in Faith.* Translated by P. T. Fuhrmann. Philadelphia, 1949.

*John Calvin: Selections from His Writings.* Edited by John Dillenberger.
Garden City, N.Y., 1971.


**Bibliographies and Surveys of Research**

*Corpus Reformatorum,* vols. 86-87, pp. 518-586. (For the period before
1900.)

Niesel, Wilhelm. *Calvin-Bibliographie 1901-1959.* Munich, 1961.

Schottenloher, see above under Luther, p. 160.

Kempff, Dionysius. *A Bibliography of Calviniana, 1959-74.* Leiden, 1975.

Scholl, Hans. *Calvinus Catholicus: Die katholische Calvinforschung im xx.
Jahrhundert.* Freiburg, 1974.

Neuser, Wilhelm H., ed. *Calvinus Theologus: Die Referate des Europäischen Kongresses für Calvinforschung vom 16. bis 19. September
1974 in Amsterdam.* Neukirchen, 1976.


**Biographies**

Benoit, Jean-Daniel. *Jean Calvin.* 2nd ed. Paris, 1948.

Cadier, Jean. *The Man God Mastered: A Brief Biography of John Calvin.*
Translated by O. R. Johnston. Grand Rapids, 1960.

Dankbaar, W. F. *Calvijn: Zijn weg en werk.* Nijkerk, 1957.

Doumergue, Emile. *Jean Calvin: Les Hommes et les choses de son temps.*
7 vols. Lausanne, 1899-1927.

Kampschulte, F. W. *Johann Calvin: Seine Kirche und sein Staat in Genf.*
2 vols. Leipzig, 1869-1899.

Neuser, Wilhelm H. *Calvin.* Berlin, 1971.

Parker, T. H. L. *Calvin: A Biography.* Philadelphia, 1975.

Staedtke, Joachim. *Johannes Calvin: Erkenntnis und Gestaltung.* Göttingen,
1969.

Stähelin, Ernst. *Johannes Calvin: Sein Leben und ausgewählte Schriften der Väter und Begründer der reformirten Kirche.* 2 vols. Elberfeld, 1863.

Wendel, Francois. *Calvin: The Origins and Development of His Religious Thought.* Translated by Philip Mairet. New York, 1963.

## Monographs

Alting von Geusau, L. G. M. *Die Lehre von der Kindertaufe bei Calvin.* Bilthoven and Mainz, 1963.

Bainton, Roland H. *Hunted Heretic: The Life and Death of Michael Servetus, 1511-1553.* Boston, 1953.

Balke, Willem. *Calvijn en de Doperse Radikalen (Calvin and the Anabaptist Radicals): With Summaries in English and German.* Amsterdam, 1973.

Barth, Karl. *Calvin.* Munich, 1936.

Barth, Peter. *Das Problem der natürlichen Theologie bei Calvin.* Munich, 1935.

Baur, Jürgen. *Gott, Recht und weltliches Regiment im Werke Calvins.* Bonn, 1965.

Beckmann, Joachim. *Vom Sakrament bei Calvin.* Tübingen, 1926.

Biéler, Andre. *La Pensée économique et sociale de Calvin.* Geneva, 1959.

Bohatec, Josef. *Bude und Calvin: Studien zur Gedankenwelt des französischen Frühhumanismus.* Graz, 1950.

———. *Calvin und das Recht.* Feudingen, 1934.

———. *Calvins Lehre von Staat und Kirche: Mit besonderer Berücksichtigung des Organismusgedankens.* Reprint ed. Aalen, 1961.

Castren, Olavi. *Die Bibeldeutung Calvins.* Helsinki, 1946.

Ganoczy, Alexandre. *Calvin: Theologien de l'Église et du ministère.* Paris, 1964.

Göhler, Alfred. *Calvins Lehre von der Heiligung.* Munich, 1934.

Grass, Hans. *Die Abendmahlslehre bei Luther und Calvin: Eine kritische Untersuchung.* 2nd ed. Gütersloh, 1954.

Hauck, Wilhelm-Albert. *Vorsehung und Freiheit nach Calvin: Ein evangelisches Glaubenszeugnis.* Gütersloh, 1947.

Jacobs, Paul. *Prädestination und Verantwortlichkeit bei Calvin.* Reprint ed. Darmstadt, 1968.

Köhler, Walter. *Züricher Ehegericht und Genfer Konsistorium.* 2 vols. Leipzig, 1932-1942.

Krusche, Werner. *Das Wirken des Heiligen Geistes nach Calvin.* Göttingen, 1957.

McDonnell, Killian. *John Calvin, the Church, and the Eucharist.* Princeton, 1967.

McNeill, John T. *The History and Character of Calvinism.* New ed. New York, 1967.

Mülhaupt, Erwin. *Die Predigt Calvins: Ihre Geschichte, ihre Form und ihre religiösen Grundgedanken.* Berlin, 1931.

Niesel, Wilhelm. *The Theology of Calvin.* Translated by Harold Knight. Philadelphia, 1956.

Pfisterer, Ernst. *Calvins Wirken in Genf.* 2nd ed. Neukirchen, 1957.

Platz, Uwe. *Calvin und Basel in den Jahren 1552-1556.* Zurich, 1974.

Reuter, Karl. *Das Grundverständnis der Theologie Calvins: Unter Einbeziehung ihrer geschichtlichen Abhängigkeiten.* Neukirchen, 1963.

Schellong, Dieter. *Calvins Auslegung der synoptischen Evangelien.* Munich, 1969.

Scholl, Hans. *Der Dienst des Gebetes nach Johannes Calvin.* Zurich, 1968.

Stadtland, Tjarko. *Rechtfertigung und Heiligung bei Calvin.* Neukirchen, 1972.

Torrance, Thomas F. *Calvin's Doctrine of Man.* New ed. Grand Rapids, 1957.

Wernle, Paul. *Calvin.* Der evangelische Glaube nach den Hauptschriften der Reformatoren, vol. 3. Tübingen, 1919.

Wolf, Hans Heinrich. *Die Einheit des Bundes: Das Verhältnis von Altem und Neuem Testament bei Calvin.* Neukirchen, 1958.